Demon-crats

Why you should never vote or even
associate with the Democrat Party
as their entire platform is not Biblical

From Abortion, America First, Border Walls,
Environmentalism, Gay Marriage, Kneeling during the Anthem,
Progressive Taxes, Sanctuary Cities, the 2nd Amendment to
Wealth Redistribution the Platform of the Democrat Party
is Contrary to the Word of God

by

THOMAS GEORGE

Thomas George is also the editor of the
conservative news website:

The Daily Manumitter Watchman

http://www.the-manumitter.com/

____

ISBN-13: 978-1729514900

ISBN-10: 1729514901

DEDICATION

I dedicate this book to Jesus Christ,
to my parents Thomas and Gloria George,
to my wife Savitrie George
and to Rush Limbaugh

without whom
this book could not have been written.

CONTENTS

PROLOGUE
WHAT ARE DEMONS?

"Satan hates you and has a terrible plan for your life. If he cannot succeed in robbing you of eternal life, he will do everything in his power to deprive you of the joy, influence, and rewards that come from serving God in this life. Since Satan cannot be in more than one place at a time, he has delegated much of his work to demons who discourage distract, and deceive through a variety of means." - Dr. Robert Jeffress

The Bible says that Lucifer in heaven was the *"seal of perfection, full of wisdom and perfect in beauty."* Lucifer became proud, he desired to be worshipped and rebelled against God. A great battle took place and Lucifer was cast out from heaven. When he fell, Lucifer took one third of the angels with him. These fallen angels are demons. Lucifer then became known as Satan. The Bible describes Satan as a spiritual evil being that opposes God. Unlike God, Satan is not omnipresent and is not able to be everywhere at the same time. As a result, he uses demons to do his work on earth and wage war against Christians. Satan and his demons oppress Christians and possess Non-Christians. How do these Demons work? It is a spiritual battle.

The Bible says, *"For we do not wrestle against flesh and blood, but against principalities, against powers, against the rulers of the darkness of this age, against spiritual hosts of wickedness in the heavenly places."* (Ephesians 6:12)

It is a battle of good versus evil. It is not a fight against people, but against demonic spirits. The Bible identifies every demonic spirit. Some of these spirits are: fear, lying, jealousy, perversion, bondage, pride, Antichrist... These spirits work together to steal, kill and destroy. In the least, they will keep believers in bondage rendering them useless in the kingdom of God. Let me give you an example. Some people have a fear of public speaking and it holds them back from reaching their potential in life. Fear of public speaking is not from God, it is demonic. The Bible says, *"For God has not given us a spirit of fear, but of power and of love and of a sound mind."* (2 Timothy 1:7)

One of the biggest tactics that Satan uses against you is deception. The Bible describes Satan as a liar and the master of all lies. He will twist the word of God to make you believe him in order that you oppose God. The Bible says Satan will even transform himself into an angel of light to deceive you. He will make evil appear good and good appear evil.

If you look at the characteristics of Satan, desiring to be worshipped, lying, appearing as an angel of light to deceive, twisting the word of God, making good appear evil and evil appear good, leading people into bondage and destruction, it the exact description of the Democrat Party. It is why I call the book Demon-crats.

I.

NEVER VOTE PERSON OVER PARTY
NEVER VOTE FOR A DEMOCRAT

Satan Appears as an Angel of Light: Vote for the person and not the political party. Voting party line is narrow minded and intolerant. Vote for a candidate based on their background, qualifications and accomplishments.

Satan's Goal: Hide the Democrat Party's true agenda which is stealing, killing and destroying.

What does the Bible say? "He who is not with Me is against Me, and he who does not gather with Me scatters abroad." (Matthew 12:30)

I have heard the argument that you should vote for the person in an election and not the political party. In fact, Ivanka Trump in an interview many years ago said, when asked if she was a Republican or Democrat, that she votes for the person and not the party. If you state otherwise, you will be labeled close minded and intolerant by Democrats. It may be why some choose not to say they vote based on the political party. However, once you know the truth of the two political parties, it is a choice between good and evil. Choosing good over evil is not close minded. I am going to start here, because I must lay the foundation for why no one should ever vote or ever be associated with the Democrat Party or any liberal organization, no matter who is representing them.

We are all Sinners

The Bible tells us that every person is a sinner. All of us have sinned in the past and will sin in the future. The definition of sin is an offense against religious or moral law. I once heard a pastor say that when he was born, the angels were sounding trumpets and there was rejoicing in all of heaven. He followed that by saying, "not really, before I was saved, I was an alcoholic, gambling, fornicator." All of us are flawed sinners…

The Bible says, *"for all have sinned and fall short of the glory of God"* (Romans 3:23).

The Bible also says that the only person to walk this earth sinless was Jesus. 1 John 3:5 says, *"and in Him (Jesus) there is no sin."* If every person is a sinner, how is one person any better than another? How do you know that the sins of the person that you are voting for in an election are less than the person you are not voting for? If that is your argument for voting for a candidate, it is not a very good argument.

Behind Closed Doors

A candidate can put on a good show in the public eye. A candidate can say a lot of things and make a lot of promises. A candidate may even have tremendous credentials. However, you can never know what a person does behind closed doors and it is not possible to know what is in a person's heart. Only God knows what is in a person's heart.

The Bible says, *"You are those who justify yourselves before men, but God knows your hearts. For what is highly esteemed among men is an abomination in the sight of God."* (Luke 16:15).

Some of the most famous people with the greatest public reputations were found out later to have done immoral and criminal acts. Comedian and actor Bill Cosby, an American icon for over 50 years, the star of the Cosby Show the #1 rated show in America during the 1980's and 1990's, was many years later accused of drugging women and having sex with them while they were unconscious. He was subsequently found guilty in a court of law.

Sports icon OJ Simpson spent decades in the public eye (as an actor and sports commentator) after a historic football career was arrested and charged with the murder of his ex-wife. Former President Bill Clinton told the American people from the White House on national television, "I did not have sex with that woman." However, he did, and it occurred in the Oval Office. Married vice president candidate John Edwards was having an affair during the 2004 presidential campaign and fathered a child with his mistress. Many Pastors have had affairs, from Jimmy Swaggart to Jim Baker. All sin and fall short of the glory of God.

There have also been many people with impeccable credentials and reputations that were disastrous leaders. Former President Jimmy Carter, by all accounts never had a personal scandal in his life (although still a sinner), was one of the worst presidents in American history. General George Patton had many known flaws, however, was known as a great military leader.

Would a person who had failed in business, filed bankruptcy and suffered a nervous breakdown be a good candidate in an election? Does that sound like a good person to vote for as president.? That person was Abraham Lincoln, one of America's greatest presidents.

Would a person who graduated from medical school, worked as an army doctor, spoke several languages and had never been divorced be a good candidate in an election? Does that sound like a good person to vote for as president? That person is Bashar al-Assad of Syria, one of the world's worst dictators.

Failure is not an End

All people sin, and all people have successes and failures. It comes with life. It starts when we are young. A child will fall many times when learning to walk. Failing comes with trying. Some of the greatest lessons can be learned from failing, sometimes even more than from succeeding. Failure shows where you need to improve and where your weaknesses are.

It is not a question if you will fail, because you will fail, but have you learned from your failure? Learning from failures leads to success. Sports teams analyze their losses to see where they failed to improve for their next game. Many people have had great success even after great failures. Dave Ramsey, probably America's foremost financial expert once filed bankruptcy. Fran Tarkenton one of the greatest quarterbacks in NFL history wrote an entire book on failure, called The Power of Failure. My greatest failures, I learned never to repeat. It is how I grew and prospered.

When Donald Trump was running for president in 2016, the liberal media and the Democrat Party focused on his business failings. Donald Trump was a billionaire who had built a worldwide real estate empire. Despite his tremendous success, his opponents focused on his business ventures that failed and they attacked him for it. There is no one that is going to be right or succeed 100% of the time and never make a mistake. Would you take Donald Trump's failures, to enjoy his success? I would!

Abraham Lincoln said, "My great concern is not whether you have failed, but whether you are content with your failure."

Zig Ziglar said, "It's not how far you fall, but how high you bounce that counts."

Vince Lombardi said, "The greatest accomplishment is not in never falling, but in rising again after you fall."

Napoleon Hill said, "Edison failed 10, 000 times before he made the electric light. Do not be discouraged if you fail a few times."

When I was young, I used to marvel at the wisdom of great quotes such as these. I thought to myself, "what great wisdom these men have!" However, it was not until after I read the Bible that I realized quotes of wisdom and truth all have root in the word of God....

The Bible says, *"For a righteous man may fall seven times And rise again."* (Proverbs 24:16)

All sin and fall short of the glory of God and all are going to fail at times. Life is filled with such events. To point out a candidate's failures is examining an election with the wrong viewpoint. John Wooden said, "The man who is afraid to risk failure seldom has to face success." Michael Jordan missed the last shot in a game many times. His career field goal percentage, (the percent of shots he made) is less than 50%. It means Michael Jordan missed more shots than he made. Lebron James lost more NBA Championship series finals than he won. Yet, these players are considered two of the NBA's greatest!

Principles Are What Matters

Principles are defined as fundamental truths that serve as the foundation for a system of beliefs. Stephen R. Covey said, "principles are rules or laws that are permanent, unchanging, and universal in nature." A person's principles, what they stand for, is of utmost importance when determining a candidate to vote for in an election.

How do you know a candidate's principles? In an election, it would be the platform of the political party they represent. The platform of a political party is the foundation of what the party stands for. A candidate representing a political party, represents that party's platform. A candidate who had failed at business, had several marriages and may not have graduated from college representing a political party with a platform against slavery is far better to support in an election than a candidate who runs a million-dollar business that graduated from Harvard representing a political party in support of slavery.

You Cannot Believe Everything You Read or Hear

There is a caveat. The platform of a political party can deceive you with rhetoric and lies. The platform can declare everything they are doing is for good, when it is not. You cannot believe everything that you read or hear. If a statement or action is not in alignment with the word of God, it is meant for harm and it is destructive. If you do not know the word of God, you must look deeper, read the fine print (look at the methods) and educate yourself on the history of results over time. You must understand, those who are opposed to God (aligned with Satan), do not have truth in them. The Bible says:

"A righteous man hates lying, But a wicked man is loathsome and comes to shame." (Proverbs 13:5)

"A faithful witness does not lie, But a false witness will utter lies." (Proverbs 14:5)

Jesus said this about Satan, *"He was a murderer from the beginning, and does not stand in the truth, because there is no truth in him. When he speaks*

a lie, he speaks from his own resources, for he is a liar and the father of it."
(John 8:44)

Satan Transforms Himself into an Angel of Light
Satan, does not only lie, but is such a master at deception he will even transform himself to appear good when he is trying to destroy you.

The Bible says, *"And no wonder! For Satan himself transforms himself into an angel of light."* (2 Corinthians 11)

The definition of deceive is to cause someone to believe something that is not true to gain some personal advantage. This is exactly what Satan does. he transforms himself to appear good, to trick you into believing something that is against the will of God. Something that is destructive to you, those around you and to society. Think of a con man who portrays himself as a business expert and comes to you with a business venture offering you the opportunity to become wealthy. He transforms into an angel of light promising financial security, however, he is deceiving you. If you just get the headlines of his message and not read the fine print (methods) and look at a history of results - you will be led down a road to destruction.

Let me give you an example: Planned Parenthood (an organization affiliated with the Democrat Party), describes itself as one of the nation's leading providers of high-quality, affordable health care, and the nation's largest provider of sex education offering "compassionate care, backed by medical experts and more than 100 years of research in reproductive health." Sounds great doesn't it? However, when you look at the method they use to accomplish their goal, it is abortion. The result over time is that Planned Parenthood commits over 300,000 abortions a year.

The Democrat Party Platform is Entirely Anti-Biblical
If you read the platform of the Democrat Party, it sounds like they stand for wonderful things. Their platform stands for building strong cities, expanding access to affordable housing, ending poverty, protecting voting rights, equality in marriage, preventing gun violence, securing reproductive health rights. It all sounds great until

you look deeper. Read the fine print, compare their methods to the word of God. I am going to prove by providing the scriptures that the Democrat Party platform is demonic and entirely not Biblical. They oppose the word of God on every issue. I will also show that the Democrat Party uses very similar tactics as Satan such as deception. I will also show that the results of Democrat Party platform over time leads to destruction.

The Democrat Party Has to Lie

The Democrat Party, like Satan must lie and deceive you. It is like the con man that I referenced above. If the con man told you the truth of what he was attempting to accomplish, you would not fall for the scheme. Instead the con man lies, deceives and sets a trap for you. If Satan or the Democrat Party told you the truth of what they were attempting to accomplish (bondage and destruction), you would not fall for their schemes. In reference to the Democrat Party, no one would never vote for them.

In 2018, Democrat Congressional candidate Tedra Cobb for New York's 21st congressional district was caught on video telling supporters that she is in favor of a certain type of gun ban. Cobb stated that if she came out in favor of the gun ban publicly, it would cause her to lose the election. Cobb said, "Well, I want you to' but, I won't win."

Not only does the Democrat Party lie about their own schemes, but they lie about their opponents. When Republican Donald Trump first announced his candidacy in 2015, up until his election and even into his presidency some of the lies Democrats said about him were that he was mentally unfit, his tax cuts would bring economic collapse, he stole the election, colluded with Russia, he would start a war with North Korea… All were lies and proven wrong in time.

Almost 40 years earlier Ronald Reagan said this about the Democrat Party, "Well, back in 1980, when I was running for president, it was all so different. Some pundits said our programs would result in catastrophe. Our views on foreign affairs would cause war. Our plans for the economy would cause inflation to soar and bring about economic collapse. I even remember one highly respected economist saying, back in 1982, that "the engines of economic growth have shut down here, and they're likely to stay that way for years to come." Well, he and the other opinion leaders were wrong. The fact is, what they called "radical" was really "right." What they called "dangerous" was just "desperately needed."

You must understand, if the Democrat Party cannot win in an election, they will try to destroy their opponents or render them useless in accomplishing their goals. It is the same tactic as Satan. After Ronald Reagan became present, the Democrat Party attacked him with the Iran Contra hearings. The Democrat Party savaged and stopped his nominee Robert Bork from becoming a justice on the Supreme Court. They attempted the same against Clarence Thomas. Today, The Democrat Party has unleashed a special counsel (appointed based on lies and fraudulent evidence) on President Donald Trump, in an attempt to destroy or neutralize his presidency, his businesses and his associates. The Democrat Party is doing the same to Brent Kavanaugh his nominee for the US Supreme Court. They will destroy anyone that opposes them.

Twisting the Word of God

In the first book of the Old Testament, Satan lied to Eve, in the Garden of Eden. His scheme was to deceive her into being disobedient to God. In the first book of the New Testament, Satan twisted the word of God, attempting to deceive Jesus to be disobedient to God. However, Jesus knew the word of God and did not fall for the lies of Satan. Man was then redeemed. This is exactly what the Democrat Party does on every issue of consequence. Be warned, when you hear a Democrat quote the Bible it will always be out of context. Democrats like Satan twist the word of God to deceive you.

The Belt of Truth

To protect against the deception and lies of Satan, it is important to know the word of God. The more you read and understand the Bible, the more you will realize how accurate and perfect the Bible is. Truth is the first thing you need to protect yourself against the schemes of Satan and it is the first piece of Armor of God. Joyce Meyer said, *"Many Christians suffer because they're too busy seeking carnal knowledge instead of the Word of God."* In the book of Ephesians, the Bible tells us to put on the full armor of God to protect against Satan.

The Bible says, *"Stand therefore, having girded your waist with truth, The belt of truth is the first piece of the armor of God."* (Ephesians 6:14).

When it comes to political issues of our time, I am going to give you the *"belt of truth"* in order that you can protect yourself against the lies of the Democrat Party. Not knowing the word of God will lead you astray in life. It will lead you down a path of bondage and destruction. By voting for candidates that support non-Biblical values it will also lead down the path to bondage and destruction of communities and countries. George Washington said, "It is impossible to rightly govern a nation without God and the Bible."

The Bible says, *"My people are destroyed for lack of knowledge.* (Hosea 4:6)

My Encounter with a Psychic

Let me give you an example... One day, after leaving the store, I found a bright beautiful colorful card on the windshield of my car advertising for psychic readings. I looked at the card and thought, "does this person know the Bible?" The Bible tells us to warn others of their sin, so I pulled out my phone and called the number on the card. A young lady answered. I asked her, "are you a Christian?" She responded, 'Very much so." I then asked her, "do you know what the Bible says about psychics?" She responded, "Yes I do! You are judging me and you are going to hell!" She then hung up the phone. This young lady told me that she knows the Bible. It's clear that she does not, or she would not be running a business as a psychic.

The Bible says, *" There shall not be found among you anyone who makes his son or his daughter pass through the fire, or one who practices witchcraft, or a soothsayer, or one who interprets omens, or a sorcerer, or one who conjures spells, or a medium, or a spiritist, or one who calls up the dead. For all who do these things are an abomination to the Lord, and because of these abominations the Lord your God drives them out from before you.* (Deuteronomy 18:10-12)

The Bible says that the activities of a psychic are an abomination to God. A person that knows the Bible would not be participating in such activities, especially to make money. Secondly, I was not judging the young lady. I was simply telling her what the Bible said about psychics. I was just telling her the word of God. She then stated that

I am going to hell. No one can ever determine who is going to hell and who is going to heaven. No one knows the entire facts of a person's life or knows what is in their heart. Only God knows such things….

When people sin, to defend it, many will say "do not judge me." Once again, people do not know scripture. There is an old saying, "do not judge a book by its cover." It means, read the book before you make a judgement about it. Get the facts, before you form an opinion. The origin of this quote is from the Bible. God is against judging by appearance. However, God is for judging when you have the facts. It is called righteous judging.

The Bible says, *"Do not judge according to appearance, but judge with righteous judgment."* (John 7:24)

My point is this young lady who advertises herself as a psychic does not know the Bible. She is twisting the word of God, is engaging in activities to make money that are contrary to the word of God and leading others as well as herself down a path to destruction.

The Bible is Truth
The Bible says the word of God is truth. As I have lived my fifty plus years on earth, I can testify to the Bible and its truth. The word of God is flawless and perfect. The Bible has been examined and dissected for thousands of years by millions of people and it cannot be disproven. When you live your life according to the Bible, it proves its truth every time.

Chuck Colson said, "The Bible's power rests upon the fact that it is the reliable, errorless, and infallible Word of God."

Leonard Ravenhill said, "God does not have to retract, revise, repair, or recall one word He has ever spoken

Norman Vincent Peale said, "The Bible - the wisest document ever known in human existence, which defies the ravages of time and change because it contains the truth that cannot be changed or invalidated."

The Bible says:

"Every word of God is pure; He is a shield to those who put their trust in Him." (Proverbs 30:5)

"Sanctify them by Your truth. Your word is truth." (John 17:17)

"All Scripture is given by inspiration of God, and is profitable for doctrine, for reproof, for correction, for instruction in righteousness, that the man of God may be complete, thoroughly equipped for every good work." (2 Timothy 3:16-17)

"Jesus said to him, "I am the way, and the truth, and the life." (John 14:6)

God has no Grey Areas

To further set the tone for this book, you must know there are no grey areas with the things that matter to God. Some candidates for office refuse to take a stand on certain issues. This is especially true of the Independent Party. It has been my habit to engage in political debate, especially with Democrats for two reasons: 1. To see what they think. 2. To show them the error in their thinking. I have heard many say regarding controversial issues, "it is not that simple, there are grey areas."

God cares about your destiny. He cares about eternity. Deciding on whether to cut your grass two or three inches high or what color to paint your house is inconsequential to God. God cares about issues that have eternal consequences. If you believe there are grey areas in the Bible, then you have not read the Bible, or you do not understand it. Every answer to the important questions of life are found in the Bible. You just have to find them. God is not a coward and there is no in between with God. He takes a stand for good against evil. There is one heaven and one hell and there is no in between.

Billy Graham said, "There are two great forces, God's force of good and the devil's force of evil."

Billy Sunday said, "God keeps no half-way house. It's either heaven or hell for you and me."

The Bible says, *"Enter by the narrow gate; for wide is the gate and broad is the way that leads to destruction, and there are many who go in by it. Because narrow is the gate and difficult is the way which leads to life, and there are few who find it."* (Matthew 7:13-14)

You Cannot Stand on the Sidelines

If you believe in grey areas, it keeps you on the sidelines. You must choose a side and there are only two sides, God's or Satan's. You are either with God or against God (for Satan).

The Bible says, *"He who is not with Me is against Me, and he who does not gather with Me scatters abroad."* (Matthew 12:30)

The Bible says if you are not working with God, you are working against Him. It means you need to be on God's side. Being neutral is being against God. I ask, do you want to oppose the God that created the heavens and earth or be on His side? God knows everything, and He knows that if Satan cannot convince you to reject God outright, he will try to neutralize by keeping you on the sidelines with lies.

Martin Luther King Jr said, "The ultimate measure of a man is not where he stands in moments of comfort and convenience, but where he stands at times of challenge and controversy."

Winston Churchill said, "Courage is the first of human qualities because it is the quality which guarantees all others."

Watchman Nee said, "God does not delight in our cowardice and withdrawal."

The Bible says, *"When I say to the wicked, 'O wicked man, you shall surely die!' and you do not speak to warn the wicked from his way, that wicked man shall die in his iniquity; but his blood I will require at your hand. Nevertheless if you warn the wicked to turn from his way, and he does not turn from his way, he shall die in his iniquity; but you have delivered your soul."* (Ezekiel 33 8-9)

The Bible says that if we can warn the wicked of their evil and do not, God will hold us accountable. However, if we warn the wicked and they do not turn from their ways, we did our part and we have delivered our soul. It is the reason that Christians speak out in opposition to issues like gay marriage and abortion. If anyone desires to persecute me for quoting scripture and defending God in this book, I say go ahead! The Bible is a higher authority than anyone desiring to persecute me. I will not stand before them when I die. I will stand before God.

The Devil, Dictators and Democrats

As I was writing this book, it came to me that the devil, dictators and democrats share similar characteristics:

1. Their goal is to be a god to people
2. They desire to be worshipped
3. They lie and twist the word of God to accomplish their goals
4. They want you dependent upon them for survival
5. They masquerade as angels of light
6. They restrict your freedoms and desire you defenseless
7. They steal, confiscate and over tax
8. They turn evil into good and good into evil
9. The result of their policies is destruction
10. They want to remove Jesus from society

The reason Democrats support and do not oppose the dictators of the world, they share the same goals. Democrat President Barrack Obama opened relations and removed sanctions against Cuba run by a dictator with no strings attached. President Barack Obama gave billions of dollars to the Iranian regime. This is a regime dedicated to the destruction of the United States and Israel.

You must understand, wealth created by commerce does not flow to the people in dictatorships, it flows to the dictator. Opening commerce to dictatorships, gives dictators more wealth and power, not the people.

Statements by the leaders of Iran regarding Republican President Donald Trump sound very similar to the Democrat Party. In fact, if you placed five statements side by side by the leaders of Iran and the leaders of the Democrat Party about President Trump, you would not be able to tell them apart. Democrats lie and counter, accusing Republican President Trump of cozying up to North Korean Dictator Kim Jung Un. President Trump has placed tough sanctions on North Korea and is opening relations with that country if they de-nuclearize.

The Result of the Democrat Platform is Destruction

The end result for people ruled by Satan, a dictatorship and Democrats is poverty, destruction and death. Below is a list of cities in America that have been run by the Democrat Party for decades:

Baltimore: One Republican mayor since 1947 (almost 70 years)
St. Louis: One Republican mayor since 1943 (almost 80 years)
Detroit: One Republican mayor since 1962 (almost 60 years)
New Orleans: One Republican mayor since 1870 (150 years)
Birmingham: Only one Republican ever served as mayor
Washington, DC: No Republican mayor since the 1800's
Milwaukee: No Republican mayor in over 100 years
Kansas City: One Republican mayor since 1930
Atlanta: The last Republican mayor was in 1877
Chicago: The last Republican mayor was in 1931

These cities all have something in common. They are filled with poverty, drugs, crime, homelessness, despair and murder. These are some of the worst cities in America and have been ruled by the Democrat Party and their policies for decades.

Elections are not a choice between two sinners. It is a choice between the two major political platforms (Republican and Democrat). One platform represents God and the other represents Satan. There was one scripture to me that describes the difference between God and Satan as well as the two major political parties in America. The words are spoken by Jesus himself.

The Bible says, *"The thief (Satan) does not come except to steal, and to kill, and to destroy. I (Jesus) have come that they may have life, and that they may have it more abundantly."* (John 10:10)

Satan steals, kills and destroys (Democrats) and Jesus gives life
and life more abundantly (Republican)... As I go through the issues,
you will see clearly that the Democrat Party aligns itself with Satan
and is in opposition to the word of God on every critical issue facing
America and the world today.

Life

II

ABORTION

Satan Appears as an Angel of Light: It is a woman's right to choose what happens with her body and that right should not be limited by government or religious authority. A pregnant woman has a right to privacy. A fetus is not a human life.

Satan's Goal: To the kill the most innocent and defenseless of all people: unborn babies.

What does the Bible say? *"These six things the Lord hates, Yes, seven are an abomination to Him: A proud look, A lying tongue, Hands that shed innocent blood."* (Proverbs 6:16-19)

I know that many people will start reading a book and then never finish it. As a result, I want to start with the topic of abortion. If you do not read anything else after this chapter, it alone should be enough that you never be associated with or place a vote for the Democrat Party. This is the most important and defining issue of our time. God requires that we take a stance on issues of importance and not remain neutral. Taxes can be raised and lowered, laws and executive orders can be overturned, but you cannot get back an innocent life once it is taken.

Democrat President Barack Obama became the first sitting president to address abortion provider Planned Parenthood. At the end of his speech, Obama said, "Thank you, Planned Parenthood. God bless you."

Democrat Nancy Pelosi said, "But it is my view that it is up to a woman to have her own right to choose the size and timing of her family."

Liberal Supreme Court Justice Ruth Bader Ginsburg said, "The emphasis must be not on the right to abortion but on the right to privacy and reproductive control."

The Three Main Lies in Support of Abortion
There are three main lies the Democrat Party uses in their support of abortion, which is the murder of an innocent life. They are:

1. It is my body and I can do with it what I please.

2. I have a right to privacy.

3. A fetus is not a human life.

All three arguments in defense of abortion are fraudulent and deceptive and easy to disprove.

It is my Body and I Can do with it what I Please
A person is not allowed to do with their body whatever they please. If what you desire to do with your body infringes on the rights of another, then your rights end. You have the right to walk down a street, however, you do not have the right to assault someone. If you assault someone, you are infringing on their rights and you will be arrested. Billy Sunday said, "I dare not exercise personal liberty if it infringes on the liberty of others."

However, this argument is founded in the lie that an unborn baby has no rights. It is founded in the lie that an unborn baby is just a mass of tissue like a tumor that must be removed, because it is dangerous to the mother (will hurt her in life).

Here are some facts… The human heart begins to beat at 18 to 21 days after fertilization; there are brain waves at six weeks and at eight weeks (two months) there are fingers and toes. On its surface, to say that an unborn baby is just a mass of tissue is absurd.

In 2018, a baby was born in an Alabama hospital weighing less than one pound. The baby survived and eventually went home from the hospital. Again, the baby was born at 22 weeks. This means this child should have been in the womb for another 4 months. When the child was born, it was not just a mass of tissue. The baby was alive and breathing with a beating heart, personality, gender and DNA.

The Right to Privacy

The second argument in support of abortion by the Democrat Party is that a pregnant woman has the right to privacy. The right to privacy emanates from the Fourth Amendment to the US Constitution. The text of the amendment states, "*The right of the people to be secure in their persons, houses, papers, and effects, against unreasonable searches and seizures, shall not be violated, and no Warrants shall issue, but upon probable cause, supported by Oath or affirmation, and particularly describing the place to be searched, and the persons or things to be seized.*"

In the 1973 case Roe v. Wade, the United States Supreme Court ruled the constitutional right to privacy included a woman's right to decide whether to have an abortion. People are imperfect, and this ruling was imperfect. As Americans, we have a constitutional right to privacy. Once if you infringe on the rights of another even within that privacy, your rights end. You have the right to privacy in your home, but do not have the right to keep someone hostage against their will. In the privacy of your home, you can play music very loud at 2 am, but the police may knock on your door and tell you to turn it down, because you are infringing on the rights of others by disturbing the peace. The right to privacy cannot be used as a defense when the rights of another are being harmed. In this case the rights of an unborn baby. Supreme Court Justice Antonin Scalia said, "The Constitution contains no right to abortion."

A Fetus is not a Human life

The Democrat Party also believes an unborn baby (with a beating heart) while still in the womb even at 9 months is just a fetus. This is an example of the deception of the Democrat Party. Do you know where the word fetus comes from? It is Latin for baby. A fetus is an unborn baby. If molecules were discovered on another planet in the solar system, it would be declared life exists! Yet, a baby with a beating heart that is in the care and protection of a mother's womb is not considered to be a life by the Democrat Party.

As a result, the Democrat Party like Satan lies and deceives. To make abortion (the murder of an innocent baby) more acceptable, Democrats change wording and meanings. Democrats change the word "baby" into "fetus." They change the word abortion into "choice" and "reproductive rights." It is done to deceive you, to make you support what is wrong in the eyes of God.

Dr. James Kennedy gave a wonderful and powerful sermon on abortion. He preached that an unborn baby has separate DNA, a separate heartbeat and is sometimes a different sex than the mother. As a result, an unborn baby is a separate life and should be treated as a separate life. He is right!

The Hypocrisy of Democrats

The Democrat Party is so deceitful they do not even believe their own lies on abortion, because their platform on protecting unborn animals like sea turtles is entirely contrary. The state of Florida provides protection against taking, possessing, disturbing, mutilating, destroying or causing to be destroyed, selling or offering for sale, transferring, molesting, or harassing any marine turtle or its nest or eggs at any time.

The Democrat Party has enacted and supports laws so as not to infringe on the rights of unborn sea turtles. Forget destroying a sea turtle egg, you cannot disturb or harass an unborn sea turtle. If you do, there are severe monetary fines and imprisonment. However, the same Democrat Party that endorses this law says an unborn baby with a beating heart has no rights. As a result, according to the Democrat Party, unborn sea turtles have more rights than unborn babies. Ann Coulter said, "Liberals are more upset when a tree is chopped down than when a child is aborted."

Republicans are Pro-Life, and Democrats are Pro-Abortion

In 2018, Iowa's Republican controlled legislature voted to outlaw abortion after a fetal heartbeat is detected. The bill was signed by the Republican governor, Kim Reynolds. However, Planned Parenthood and the Iowa branch of the American Civil Liberties Union (both liberal and Democrat Party supporting organizations) sued to stop the law from coming into effect.

Man's Standards are Flawed

Democrat standards are flawed when it comes to the concept of life. Not only do they have different standards for unborn babies and unborn sea turtles, but they have different standards as to when life ends (a beating heart), and when life begins (not a beating heart, but the intention of the mother). When a heartbeat is no longer detected a person is declared dead. To the Democrat Party that is not the standard as to when a life begins. This inconsistency shows that man's standards are flawed. The truth is always found in the Bible and God's standard is perfect.

The Bible says, *"Before I formed you in the womb I knew you; Before you were born I sanctified you; I ordained you a prophet to the nations."* (Jeremiah 1:5).

The Bible Reveals Truths we are now Learning

The Bible says that God knows you before you were even formed in the womb. It also says that before you were born He sanctified you, which means set us apart for His use. Clearly, we are a person while in the womb. The Bible reveals truths that are proven with time. Studies in the last decades show that a baby can hear and feel in the womb. There are studies that show babies can even learn while in the womb. Although, this was just discovered, the Bible described this two thousand years ago.

The Bible says, *"And it happened, when Elizabeth heard the greeting of Mary, that the babe leaped in her womb; and Elizabeth was filled with the Holy Spirit. Then she spoke out with a loud voice and said, 'Blessed are you among women, and blessed is the fruit of your womb! But why is this granted to me, that the mother of my Lord should come to me? For indeed, as soon as the voice of your greeting sounded in my ears, the babe leaped in my womb for joy."* (Luke 1:41- 44)

The Bible says, *"the babe leaped"* while in the womb for joy at the sound of a greeting.

Partial-Birth Abortion is Evil

If the abortion of an unborn baby in the womb was not wicked enough, the Democrat Party platform supports of one of the evilest practices ever devised by man and that is partial-birth abortion. The arguments in support of this practice by the Democrat Party are once again completely deceptive. It is a testament of how lawless, evil and anti-God the Democrat Party platform is. It illustrates how far they will go to murder an innocent unborn baby.

Partial-birth abortion is the taking the life (murder) of a baby as it is being born. Hence the term, partial-birth. It means as a baby is partially born and then its innocent life is taken away (murdered). Democrat President Barack Obama before becoming president supported a bill mandating if an abortion procedure failed and a baby was born and not aborted, the baby should be left to die on the operating table, because the original intention of the mother was abortion. That is horrifying! Imagine leaving a newborn baby to just die on a table! Cruel and evil does not go far enough to describe this!

Health vs Life in the Partial-Birth Abortion Debate

The Democrat Party in order to deceive and mask their evil, say they only supports partial-birth abortion when the mother's health is in danger. They do not want, "anything to happen to the mother." As a result, if a mother's health is in danger, according to the Democrat Party, it is okay to have partial-birth abortion. Sounds good doesn't it?

It is not good! It is so deceptive that most people believe it and do not realize they are being deceived. Satan appears as an angel of light! First, let me state that the Republican Party platform is that partial birth abortion should only be used in the rare case that a mother's life is in danger. Compare the two platforms... Democrats believe in taking the life of the unborn when a mother's health is in danger, Republicans believe in taking the life of the unborn when a mother's life is in danger...

Taking a Life when your Health is in Danger is Murder

A "mother's health in danger" can mean almost anything or any circumstance. It is vague and not precise. Stress can put health in danger. The common cold puts health in danger. When it comes to taking a life, there should be no vagueness, only preciseness. Nowhere in society are you allowed to take the life of another when only your health is in danger. Taking a life when your health is in danger is called murder! Rush Limbaugh said, "I believe that life begins at conception and that killing that human life is justifiable only when it's necessary to save the mother's life."

The Law of Self Defense

The sixth commandment says that *"you shall not murder."* Murder is defined as killing of an innocent person. What is abortion? It is the killing of an innocent and defenseless baby! It is murder! Let me explain the difference between murder and killing. If an intruder broke into your home and attempted to kill your children and you shot them dead, it is not murder. You killed someone defending your own life and the lives of your children. If you did not stop the intruder and you or your children are killed that is murder.

The law of self-defense says that you are only allowed to take a life (use deadly force) when your life, not your health, becomes endangered. It originates from the Bible in the Old Testament. If you applied the standard that the Democrat Party uses with abortion to all of society, it would mean that it would be lawful to kill someone sitting next to you with the flu, because your health is danger. If you felt stress because your boss is treating you unfairly at work, it would be lawful to kill your boss. The result would be chaos, destruction and death everywhere in society.

The George Zimmerman Trial

There was a very publicized national case that occurred in Florida. George Zimmerman was charged with second-degree murder in the shooting death of 17-year-old Trayvon Martin. George Zimmerman was a security guard and got into an altercation with Travon Martin at a housing complex. A witness stated that he saw Travon Martin on top of George Zimmerman beating him like they do in a mixed martial arts match. George Zimmerman believed his life was in danger and that his gun might be taken from him and used against him. During the altercation, Zimmerman grabbed his gun and shot Travon Martin killing him. Democrats and liberals marched and protested, calling Zimmerman's actions murder. Zimmerman was subsequently found not guilty.

Once again, if you use the Democrat Party standard relating to partial birth abortion (that it is okay to kill when your health is in danger), there should not have been one single argument or protest. Democrats who support partial birth abortion (taking the life of an innocent defenseless baby) with the standard of a mother's health in danger were wearing hoodies in support of Travon Martin, who was violently attacking George Zimmerman.

What does the Bible say about Abortion?
The Bible says that God hates abortion. The Bible is explicit in this matter.

The Bible says, *"These six things the Lord hates, Yes, seven are an abomination to Him: A proud look, A lying tongue, Hands that shed innocent blood."* (Proverbs 6:16-17)

The Bible says God hates hands that shed innocent blood. There is nothing more innocent than an unborn child. Anyone in support of abortion is supporting something that God hates. No matter what man or a political party may call it, "choice" or "reproductive rights", supporting abortion is opposing the word of God.

Before becoming president, Democrat Barack Obama in defense of abortion stated referring to his own children, "if they make a mistake, I don't want them punished with a baby." Obama believes having children is punishment. Let me tell you what the Bible says….

The Bible says *"Behold, children are a heritage from the Lord, The fruit of the womb is a reward."* (Psalm 127:3)

The Bible says that children are a blessing and a reward. God trusts you with children to care for them until they become adults. Most problems with children, result from bad parenting or no parenting at all. If you raise your children with Democrat values, you are going to have problems. I had great parents with conservative values. I never saw them fight, heard them curse, they never hit me, they never got arrested, they worked hard, aged gracefully and they instilled hard work, discipline and respect in me.

The Bible says, *"Train up a child in the way he should go, And when he is old he will not depart from it."* (Proverbs 22:6)

I loved my parents dearly. I long to see them again one day.

When my mother got Alzheimer's Disease, I took care of her as long as I could and protected her until she passed away. She was able to live in her home for many more years. She was a great parent and raised a son that honored her. Who knows what would have happened to her, if I did not help and care for her in her old age. Children are a blessing from the Lord.

Hurting the Least of These is like Hurting Jesus

Lastly, there are many in the Democrat Party who believe that a baby should be aborted because they have a developmental disability such Down's Syndrome, Cerebral Palsy... This takes the murder of an unborn baby to an even more wicked level. Democrats believe not only is it okay to murder an innocent unborn defenseless baby as it is being born, but it is okay to murder an innocent unborn defenseless baby with disabilities.

What does the Bible say about how you treat those with disabilities? Let me preface that answer by telling you what the Bible says about relationships with others. The Sixth Commandment says, to *"honor your mother and father and your days will be long on this earth."* Bible also says, *"to love your neighbor as yourself."* However, there is only one group of individuals the Bible says that your actions toward them is like doing it to Jesus Himself. That group is the, *"least among us".* The definition of least is lowest in importance or position. Whatever you do to the lowest, weakest and most vulnerable in society (whether good or bad) is like doing it to Jesus himself.

Mother Theresa said, "I see God in every human being. When I wash the leper's wounds, I feel I am nursing the Lord himself. Is it not a beautiful experience?"

Smith Wigglesworth said, "I am never happier in the Lord than when I am in a bedroom with a sick person."

The Bible says, *"Then the righteous will answer Him (Jesus), saying, 'Lord, when did we see You hungry and feed You, or thirsty and give You drink? When did we see You a stranger and take You in, or naked and clothe You? Or when did we see You sick, or in prison, and come to You?' And the King will answer and say to them, 'Assuredly, I say to you, inasmuch as you did it to one of the least of these My brethren, you did it to Me."* (Matthew 25:37-40)

This Bible says that when you go out of your way to help the most vulnerable in society, it is like helping Jesus. However, the scripture goes on and says that when you ignore the most vulnerable it is like turning your back on Jesus. The Bible says, *"Then He will also say to those on the left hand, 'Depart from Me, you cursed, into the everlasting fire prepared for the devil and his angels: for I was hungry and you gave Me no food; I was thirsty and you gave Me no drink; I was a stranger and you did not take Me in, naked and you did not clothe Me, sick and in prison and you did not visit Me.' 'Then they also will answer Him, saying, 'Lord, when did we see You hungry or thirsty or a stranger or naked or sick or in prison, and did not minister to You?' Then He will answer them, saying, 'Assuredly, I say to you, inasmuch as you did not do it to one of the least of these, you did not do it to Me.' And these will go away into everlasting punishment, but the righteous into eternal life."* (Matthew 25:41-46)

The Scripture tells us that that those that help the lowest and most vulnerable in society are given eternal life, while those that turn their back on them are given eternal punishment. Unborn children in the womb are the most innocent and defenseless in society. They cannot protect themselves and they have no voice. They qualify as the least and most vulnerable among us. By aborting unborn children, they are not only being ignored, they are being murdered. According to scripture, aborting unborn children and unborn children with disabilities in the womb, would be like murdering Jesus Himself. It is consistent with the Democrat Party platform that wants to remove Jesus from society.

Individuals with Disabilities Teach you Love

I spent many years in financial services, not knowing the word of God. After I dedicated my life to the Lord, I left the world of finance and started doing ministry. I took a part time job working with individuals with developmental disabilities. Before I started working with these individuals, my thoughts were not as they are now. Whatever my thinking was, it was wrong…

My first day at work at a "Day Program" (a place where individuals with developmental disabilities go to work, earn money for themselves and find fellowship), I will never forget. There was a dance taking place that day. My first sight was a tall black male with disabilities dancing in the middle of the room surrounded by dozens of others with developmental disabilities. It is difficult to describe, but his motions were jerky, and his face was contorting. It was unlike anything I had ever seen, but he was dancing, smiling and having fun.

I learned with time that this young man had a job working in the woodshop. He cut points on the ends of short and long pieces of wood using a miter saw that were then sold as boundary markers to survey companies. He could not speak but understood everything that you said to him. I would fill in at the woodshop at times and I got to know him well. He was a hard worker. He was not paid much, however, he loved his job! He was always helping with anything that needed to be done around the woodshop. He was one of the nicest and gentlest people that you would ever meet. I used to tell him, "sit down, it is okay, take a break", because he worked so hard.

And there was another young man that worked in the woodshop that had Downs Syndrome. He was very high functioning. He was another hard worker. He would see me every day, give me a high five and a hug. He would say, "Hi, Thomas how are you?", in the softest voice. He would always tell me that he missed me in the woodshop. He was the sweetest gentlest person you would ever meet in your life. What an outstanding person this young man was....

And there was another young lady with Down's Syndrome. Despite her disability, she was outgoing, happy and always positive. One hour around her, would change your life forever! She had such a positive outlook on life… We would take groups on outings into the community, especially to this one large thrift store. When this young lady walked in the store, she was a star. She knew everyone, and everyone knew her. I can tell you that I go to the same places and not one person knows my name or who I am….

And there was another young man, JP. He had more advanced Down Syndrome and barely ever spoke. However, he always smiled at you and he understood everything you said. I would always give him a pat on the back and he would always give me the biggest smile. One of the few times I ever heard him speak was after I gave a message at our Christmas Party about the true meaning of Christmas. JP walked up to me shook my hand and said, "God bless you". He was a gentle soul.

And then there was HO, that was his initials. I called him H2O - because he had twice as much energy as anyone I had ever met in my life. H20 is also the symbol for water and water is necessary for life. HO was life. When he walked into a room, he brought life to the room. He had so much energy. He was always in a good mood and always dancing. He loved to talk. He would always have a crush on one of the girl workers. I loved H20 like a brother. We called each brother!

I could give you 100 wonderful stories of 100 different individuals with developmental disabilities. I came to realize in time that these individuals (many who could not read or write), did something much greater for society than hold a job and pay taxes. They teach you to love unconditionally and appreciate everything that you have. They were happy just to have you as a friend. They teach you that things (possessions) do not matter, it is people and relationships that really matter in life. They demonstrate that love is the greatest gift and without love you have nothing. It is probably the reason many in the Democrat Party do not believe individuals with developmental disabilities have the right to live.

The Bible says, *"Though I speak with the tongues of men and of angels, but have not love, I have become sounding brass or a clanging cymbal. And though I have the gift of prophecy, and understand all mysteries and all knowledge, and though I have all faith, so that I could remove mountains, but have not love, I am nothing. And though I bestow all my goods to feed the poor, and though I give my body to be burned, but have not love, it profits me nothing."* (1 Corinthians 13:1-3)

The Democrat Party as an Organization should be Extinct
The Democrat Party portrays itself as a party of compassion, yet they support the murder of unborn innocent babies and unborn innocent babies with disabilities. How is this compassion? I ask you would you really want to be part and be proud of an organization that supports such evil activity?

No person should ever be associated with the Klu Klux Klan, they have murdered innocent people based on race. No person should ever want to be associated with the Nazi Party, they murdered innocent people based on nationality. The same is for true for the Democrat Party. No person should ever be associated with the Democrat Party, as they support the murder of innocent unborn children as they are being born, including those with disabilities. The

Democrat Party, as an organization, should be extinct and in the same class as the Klu Klux Klan and the Nazi Party.

Calling what is Evil Good and Calling Good Evil

When you take something that is good and turn it to evil and take something evil and turn it to good, it is the perversion of what God intends. Bernie Sanders who ran as a Democrat in the 2016 presidential election said, "I am for abortion and against the death penalty." State Attorney for the Ninth Judicial Circuit Court of Florida Aramis Ayala (a Democrat) refused to pursue the death penalty on capital murder cases she was assigned to, including against a man who allegedly murdered his pregnant girlfriend and a policeman. Republican Governor Rick Scott subsequently had her removed from all capital cases.

Support of abortion and opposition to the death penalty is a consistent position across the Democrat Party. The death penalty (known as capital punishment) is administered against those who have been found guilty of a serious crime in a court of law. They are guilty of a capital crime. Contrast this with the Democrat position on abortion. They are for putting to death an innocent unborn child guilty of no crime. The Democrat Party is for saving the life of the guilty and for the murder of the innocent. These positions are contrary to the word of God.

The Bible says, *"Woe to those who call evil good, and good evil; Who put darkness for light, and light for darkness; Who put bitter for sweet, and sweet for bitter!"* (Isaiah 5:20)

The word *"woe"* in the Bible is a serious warning from God that there will be judgement for an action. The scripture says God is warning do not call evil good and good evil or you will face severe consequences.

III

THE SECOND AMENDMENT
THE RIGHT TO BEAR ARMS

Satan Appears as an Angel of Light: If there were no guns, there would be peace. The Second Amendment does not give citizens the right to keep and bear arms, but only allows for the states to keep a militia. Individuals do not need guns for protection; it is the role of local and federal government to protect the people through law enforcement agencies and the military.

Satan's Goal: Prevent innocent people from defending themselves against crimes like robbery, rape and murder. Prevent people from defending against a tyrannical government. Prevent a Christian country from defending against enemies.

What does the Bible say? *"Then He said to them, "But now, he who has a money bag, let him take it, and likewise a knapsack; and he who has no sword, let him sell his garment and buy one."* (Luke 22:36)

The Second Amendment was ratified by Congress in 1791 and is one of 10 amendments that form the Bill of Rights. The text of the Second Amendment reads: "A well-regulated Militia, being necessary to the security of a free State, the right of the people to keep and bear Arms, shall not be infringed."

The debate over time has been, what is the meaning of the Second Amendment? Is the Second Amendment talking about only militias having the right to bear arms or does it include all citizens? The answer is simple, the Second Amendment says, "the right of the people to keep and bear Arms, shall not be infringed." The text is specific! Alexander Hamilton, one of the Founding Fathers of the United States, said, "The constitution shall never be construed...to prevent the people of the United States who are peaceable citizens from keeping their own arms." However, it has been the agenda of the Democrat Party to limit or end the right to bear arms.

Democrat President Back Obama said, "I don't believe people should be able to own guns."

Democrat presidential candidate Hillary Clinton said, "The Supreme Court is wrong on the Second Amendment. And I am going to make that case every chance I get."

California Democrat Senator Dianne Feinstein said, "Banning guns addresses a fundamental right of all Americans to feel safe."

Three Reasons for the Second Amendment
1. To protect against foreign invaders.
2. To protect you from a tyrannical government
3. To protect your family and personal property from criminals.

To Protect Against Foreign Invaders
The 2nd Amendment is the result of the Revolutionary War. In 1776, with the signing of the Declaration of Independence, the original thirteen colonies declared their independence from Great Britain. After it was signed, it did not mean the colonies were free. Great Britain was opposed to the declared independence of the colonies. As a result, war broke out in North America between the colonies and an invading Great Britain. Men of the colonies banded together with guns to protect their families, property and the colonies against the invasion. It was the result of individuals fighting back with guns that led to the defeat of Great Britain and independence of the colonies. Some day in the future, America, may be invaded again by a hostile country. Citizens may have to band together with guns to fight to protect their families, property and their country.

To Protect Against a Tyrannical Government
It is the Democrat Party that desires to limit or ban guns. Once again, it is something they have in common with the dictators of the

world. Uganda implemented gun control in 1970's under dictator Idi Amin. From 1971 to 1979, over 300,000 Christians, unable to defend themselves, were rounded up and murdered. Cambodia under the dictator Pol Pot, was responsible for killing one million of his own unarmed citizens.

Russian dictator Joseph Stalin said, "If the opposition (citizen) disarms, well and good. If it refuses to disarm, we shall disarm it ourselves."

To Protect Family and Personal Property from Criminals

The police and military cannot be everywhere to protect citizens. Citizens need to have the ability to protect themselves against criminals and evil. Most Americans are hardworking, honest and law-abiding people. You must understand, because something is illegal, it does not mean that it is completely removed from society. Drugs such as cocaine, heroin and Methamphetamines are illegal in America, but can easily be obtained in just about every city across the country, because they are smuggled in across the border. Prisons should be the most secure environments in the world, with armed guards and secure border walls. However, drugs are still rampant in prisons, because they are also smuggled in. The same would be true for guns in America, even if guns were outlawed. Do you know who would possess guns if they were outlawed? It would only be criminals. As a result, the innocent law-abiding person would be left defenseless.

France has almost a complete ban on guns in society. There is no right to bear arms. To own a gun in France, you need a hunting license which needs to be renewed and requires a psychological evaluation. However, Terrorists killed 89 people in a concert in 2015. In England, access to firearms is tightly controlled and handguns are outlawed. However, in 2018 a record number of murders have been committed with guns and knives.

Refuting Another Liberal Argument

There is also the argument that innocent people are killed accidentally by guns. Accidental deaths do occur with guns every year. It is a sad fact that people die in accidents. People are flawed and make mistakes. It is not possible to prevent all accidental deaths.

People slip and fall, choke on food, are killed by pet dogs and drown... The number of yearly deaths caused by automobile accidents is staggering. More than 40,000 people die in automobile accidents each year in America. This number dwarfs the number of accidental gun related deaths. If we are to apply the logic the Democrat Party uses in their desire to remove guns from society, automobiles would have to be outlawed and there be a complete ban on driving.

America is a Nation of Laws

America is a nation of laws. If an elected public official or even a private citizen disagrees with the Constitution, they cannot just arbitrarily change it. There is a process for amending the Constitution and it is not easy one. The Founding Fathers established the Republic that way to prevent someone from coming into a political office, abusing their power and changing the foundation of the country. It is the reason that America has three branches of government. The Founders saw the history of abuse of power by the kings of England. They wanted a government decentralized with power given to the people. As a result, it is no easier to change the second amendment as it is to change the first amendment, which guarantees the freedom of speech.

Harvard Law Professor Alan Dershowitz said, "Foolish liberals who are trying to read the Second Amendment out of the Constitution by claiming it's not an individual right or that it's too much of a public safety hazard, don't see the danger in the big picture. They're courting disaster by encouraging others to use the same means to eliminate portions of the Constitution they don't like."

Democrats Twist the Word of God

Referring to gun control and the second amendment, Democrats will cite the scripture in the book of Matthew when Jesus says to turn the other cheek.

The Bible says, *"You have heard that it was said, 'An eye for an eye and a tooth for a tooth.' But I tell you not to resist an evil person. But whoever slaps you on your right cheek, turn the other to him also. If anyone wants to sue you and take away your tunic, let him have your cloak also. And whoever compels you to*

*go one mile, go with him two. Give to him who asks you, and from him who
wants to borrow from you do not turn away."* (Matthew 5:38-42)

This scripture is taken completely out of context relating to gun
control. If someone desires to slap me, or take from me and my life
not in danger, I will let them do it and not fight back… If someone
wants to borrow from me, I will give. However, this scripture does
not address the occurrence of someone breaking into a home to
murder you and your family. It is not addressing violent crime. If
someone breaks into my home and wants to kill me or my family, I
will not turn the other cheek. I will take out my gun and protect my
family.

The Bible is specific. The Words of God are exact. You cannot
add to it or subtract from it…

The Bible says, *"Whatever I command you, be careful to observe it; you
shall not add to it nor take away from it."* (Deuteronomy 12:32)

Bearing Arms is Biblical
What does the Bible say about bearing Arms? Regardless of what
any pundit, editorial or politician says, bearing arms for personal
protection is Biblical. Anyone against the right to bear arms is
opposing the word of God. Before Jesus went to the cross, He
instructed his disciples to sell some of their items and buy side arms
(swords).

The Bible says, *"And He (Jesus) said to them, "When I sent you without
money bag, knapsack, and sandals, did you lack anything?" So they said,
"Nothing." Then He (Jesus) said to them, "But now, he who has a money bag,
let him take it, and likewise a knapsack; and he who has no sword, let him sell
his garment and buy one. For I say to you that this which is written must still be
accomplished in Me: 'And He was numbered with the transgressors. 'For the
things concerning Me have an end." So they said, "Lord, look, here are two
swords." And He (Jesus) said to them, "It is enough."* (Luke 22:35-38)

Jesus commanded His disciples to sell some of their possessions
and buy swords. Swords were the sidearms of that day. There are
only two reasons for someone to possess a sword (sidearm/weapon).

The first would be for offensive purposes and the second would be for defensive purposes. So why did Jesus tell His disciples to buy swords, was it for offensive or defensive purposes?

Jesus is the Prince of Peace

Jesus was referred to by many names in the Bible. One of those names comes from the book of Isaiah. The prophet Isaiah referred to Jesus as the Prince of Peace.

The Bible says, *"For unto us a Child is born, Unto us a Son is given; And the government will be upon His shoulder. And His name will be called Wonderful, Counselor, Mighty God, Everlasting Father, Prince of Peace."* (Isaiah 9:6)

K.P. Yohannan said, "Love was the bedrock of Jesus' life, the very reason He came to seek and save the lost."

Charles Finney said, "Let it then be understood that Christ came in human flesh to reveal before our eyes the great love of God."

Jesus, the Prince of Peace, said *to love your neighbor as yourself* and *to love others as He loved.* Jesus did not say to take vengeance on your enemies. He said to *love your enemies* and *to pray for those who persecute you.* Jesus also said to *forgive* those who hurt you. The entire earthly ministry of Jesus was about love and forgiveness. It would go against all the Jesus taught for Him to command His disciples to purchase swords for offensive purposes.

Jesus Warned of Persecution for Preaching the Gospel

Jesus knew the disciples would suffer persecution and would need to protect themselves while preaching the Gospel. Jesus warned of it. He told the disciples that they would be hated for preaching the Gospel and when they were persecuted, He said to flee to another city. Jesus did not command them to stay and fight.

The Bible says, *"And you will be hated by all for My name's sake. But he who endures to the end will be saved. When they persecute you in this city, flee to another. For assuredly, I say to you, you will not have gone through the cities of Israel before the Son of Man comes."* (Matthew 10:22-23)

Put your Sword into the Sheath

The arrest of Jesus in the Garden of Gethsemane gives further evidence the disciples had swords for defensive purposes. When Jesus was arrested, Peter took out his sword and attacked a Roman soldier. Peter missed the soldiers head and cut off the ear of the soldier. What did Jesus say to Peter?

The Bible says, *"So Jesus said to Peter, Put your sword into the sheath. Shall I not drink the cup which My Father has given Me?"* (John 18:11)

Jesus told Peter to return the sword back to its place (sheath). Jesus did not tell Peter to throw the sword away.

In a parallel verse (recorded in Matthew) the Bible says, *"But Jesus said to him, "Put your sword in its place, for all who take the sword will perish by the sword. Or do you think that I cannot now pray to My Father, and He will provide Me with more than twelve legions of angels? How then could the Scriptures be fulfilled, that it must happen thus?"* (Matthew 26: 52)

Once again, Jesus said to put the sword in its place. He also said those who take the sword will perish by it. It is a clear message that the sword should not be used an offensive weapon.

The Hypocrisy of Democrats

Democrat politicians and liberal celebrities hold rallies and use social media to denounce gun rights and the Second Amendment whenever there is tragedy involving a gun. However, it is these same Democrats and liberals who have armed bodyguards protecting them when they are out in public at such events.

A Just God Wants the Innocent Protected

The Bible is clear that Jesus told the disciples to purchase swords for self-defense to protect themselves against evil. The Democrat Party once again is in opposition to the word of God. They align with Satan in wanting to give an advantage to evil and leave the innocent unarmed and vulnerable. Criminals will always obtain guns even if they are outlawed and their purpose for owning guns is not defensive, but offensive (to commit crimes). Satan desires to slaughter the innocent whether it is you, your family or an unborn baby. The Democrat Party platform on the second amendment is not Biblical and assists evil that desire to steal, kill and destroy.

IV

LEGALIZATION OF MARIJUANA AND OTHER MIND-ALTERING DRUGS

Satan Appears as an Angel of Light: Legalization of recreational marijuana has beneficial effects and is a source of tax revenue and jobs. Alcohol is legal and marijuana is better than alcohol.

Satan's Goal: To destroy your mind and body or even kill you. In the least, steal from you, leave you homeless, imprisoned or render you useless in the Kingdom of God.

What does the Bible say? *"Do you not know that you are the temple of God and that the Spirit of God dwells in you? If anyone defiles the temple of God, God will destroy him. For the temple of God is holy, which temple you are."* (1 Corinthians 3:16-17)

The first chapter in this section demonstrates that the Democrat Party is in support of the taking the lives of innocent unborn babies. The second chapter in this section demonstrates the Democrat Party is in support of disarming innocent people, leaving them defenseless against criminals intending harm. I have included the legalization of drugs in this section as the Democrat Party supports mind-altering drugs that destroy and takes lives. The testimony of those who use or sell drugs for any extended period is that you will end up homeless, in prison or dead. There is nothing to be gained with the legalization of marijuana for recreational use.

Democrat President Barack Obama said, "And I am not somebody who believes that legalization is a panacea. But I do believe that treating this as a public-health issue, the same way we do with cigarettes or alcohol, is the much smarter way to deal with it."

Democrat Senator Cory Booker said, "This [prohibition] makes no sense in science, makes no sense in compassion, makes no sense in terms of law, it makes no sense frankly in terms of economics."

Liberal Noam Chomsky said, "Legalizing marijuana would make a lot of sense, I don't think there's a single case of marijuana overdose on record and tens of millions of users. It's much less dangerous than alcohol, for example."

The following reasons are what Democrats cite to argue in support of the legalization of recreational marijuana. These reasons are easy to refute.

1. The majority of the public is in favor of legalization
2. Marijuana being illegal is too expensive for our justice system
3. It's a potentially new source of revenue and jobs
4. It's not a gateway drug
5. Marijuana is a natural plant
6. Marijuana is used to alleviate many medical conditions

Majority of the Public are in Favor of Legalization
There have been many activities in America that at one time were supported by a majority of people and legal. However, those activities are now considered not only illegal, but immoral. Some obvious ones are slavery, a woman's right to vote and discrimination against people of color. The legalization argument, because a majority support something is fraudulent. Using this logic, if a majority of people support putting to death all individuals with a disability, then it would be legal to do so. It is a fraudulent argument.

Drugs have become acceptable and almost common place in society today, but it does not mean it is acceptable in the eyes of God. It is the reason that God gave us His Word. Creflo Dollar said, "Just because something is accepted does not make it acceptable in God's eyes." The Bible tells us not to conform to the world. Conform means to act in accordance with prevailing standards or customs.

The Bible says, *"I beseech you therefore, brethren, by the mercies of God, that you present your bodies a living sacrifice, holy, acceptable to God, which is your reasonable service. And do not be conformed to this world, but be transformed by the renewing of your mind, that you may prove what is that good and acceptable and perfect will of God."* (Romans 12:1-2)

The Bible says we are to give our bodies as a living sacrifice to God. We are to do what is good, pleasing and acceptable to Him.

Marijuana being Illegal is too Expensive to our Justice System

This is another fraudulent argument. It ignores that there are other remedies for marijuana possession than placing offenders in jail. The penalty for possession of illegal drugs can be a ticket (fine) rather than imprisonment. The penalty for dealing drugs can be imprisonment.

Many people do not use marijuana for the simple fact it is illegal. Being illegal is a deterrent, even if it is a fine. Once it becomes legal, many will experiment with it because the government is saying that it is okay. I began drinking alcohol at age 19 because it was legal to do so. In my late teens and early twenties, marijuana was offered to me many times at parties. However, I never tried it simply because it was illegal. If it was legal, it is very possible that I would have experimented with it.

It's a Potentially New Source of Revenue and Jobs

Legalization of marijuana as a method to generate tax revenue is absurdity. Giving a wasteful overspending government more money is the equivalent of giving a drug addict more drugs and saying it is good for them. Government spending more is a way for the government to entrap more people on handouts and dependence. It would be better for government to refrain from wasteful and excessive spending. Period!

Marijuana is a Natural Plant

There is the argument there is nothing wrong with smoking a natural plant. There is a plant called Coca (Erythroxylum coca). Cocaine derives from the leaves in the coca plant. If you are going to use the argument that marijuana should be legal because it is a natural plant, then you would have to use the same argument for cocaine. Also, there are other natural plants that if eaten or smoked are deadly, such as oleander.

Marijuana is not a Gateway Drug

Many say that marijuana is not a gateway drug. For some it is a gateway drug, but for others it is not. Cory Monteith, a young actor from Canada, died at the age of 31 from drug abuse. Before his death, he gave an interview and said that marijuana was a gateway drug for him. Marijuana was the start and from there he graduated to heroin and other drugs. Many have claimed that their drug addiction began after using marijuana. As a result, Marijuana is a gateway drug.

Marijuana is Used to Alleviate Many Medical Conditions

There is a big push today, not just for the legalizing recreational marijuana, but for medical marijuana. As of 2018, more than 30 states have legalized medical marijuana. The argument for medical marijuana is that it helps relieve pain for individuals who are suffering. In this age of medical wonder, for every disease and disorder that marijuana has been recommended, there are alternatives. There are medications that you can take that do not affect others around you like marijuana smoke does.

It is important that you know the tactics of Satan. There is a phrase, "give them an inch and they take a mile." That is exactly what Satan does. The Bible says in Ephesians, *"give no place to the devil."* If you give the devil an inch, he will take a mile. The legalization of drugs such as marijuana, begins with legalization for medical use. However, what soon follows is legalization for recreational use.

This tactic is occurring currently with legalized medical marijuana. To get a medical prescription from a doctor, there must be a diagnosed medical condition. To get a prescription for high blood pressure, a person must have the condition of high blood pressure.

A prescription for a medication is specific to that medical condition. However, if you look at the qualifying list of conditions for medical marijuana, it is pretty much any condition at all… To be able to smoke medical marijuana in Florida the list of conditions includes, "anxiety, chronic pain/severe pain, irritable bowel syndrome, migraines, muscle spasms, post-traumatic stress disorder, severe

nausea or any other ailment/condition of the same
severity/symptoms, when determined by a physician's opinion that
the medical use of marijuana would surpass any potential health
risks." Basically, if you get headaches, a backache, a stomach ache, are
stressed out, have pain or anything a doctor determines, you can get a
prescription to smoke marijuana.

Democrats Twist the Word of God

Democrats once again twist the word of God and cite the Bible in
support of their agenda of marijuana legalization. The Scripture they
cite is the following.... *"And God said, "See, I have given you every
herb that yields seed which is on the face of all the earth, and every tree whose fruit
yields seed; to you it shall be for food."* (Genesis 1:29)

The Bible says, God gave us every herb, and every tree whose
fruit yields seed for food, it does not say for smoking. God always
gives us goodness and it is Satan that perverts it. He will take what is
meant for good and pervert it to something bad.

What Does the Bible Say about Drug Use?

The Bible does not mention specific drugs to avoid by name. The
reason is that if the Bible did, as new drugs were created people
would say, well the Bible does not say you cannot do Molly, Ecstasy
or some new designer drug. Satan is always creating new mind-
altering drugs to destroy lives and kill. The Bible, however, is specific
when it speaks of remaining sober.

The Bible says, *"Be sober, be vigilant; because your adversary the devil
walks about like a roaring lion, seeking whom he may devour."* (1 Peter 5:8).

The Bible says to be sober. The definition of sober is: freedom
from intoxication. The Bible also tells us to be vigilant. The definition
of vigilant is: to be especially watchful, because Satan is looking to
devour (prey upon) you. Drugs that alter the mind, whether they are
legal, or illegal are warned against by God. I have listened to
Christians debate whether it is okay to drink alcohol or not. Again,
the Bible warns of insobriety. As a result, it is okay to have a small
glass of wine or even a beer if it does not lead to insobriety.
However, again drinking alcohol to intoxication is not okay. Billy

Sunday said, "The saloon is a liar. It promises good cheer and sends sorrow." The Bible says, give no place to the devil. It would be wise to avoid alcohol altogether.

The Bible says, *"Wine is a mocker, Strong drink is a brawler, And whoever is led astray by it is not wise."* (Proverbs 20:1)

The Bible also says, *"For the grace of God that brings salvation has appeared to all men, teaching us that, denying ungodliness and worldly lusts, we should live soberly, righteously, and godly in the present age, looking for the blessed hope and glorious appearing of our great God and Savior Jesus Christ, who gave Himself for us, that He might redeem us from every lawless deed and purify for Himself His own special people, zealous for good works."* (Titus 2:11-14)

The Consequence of Sin can Last a Lifetime
Sin is disobedience to the word of God and the Bible warns against it. The Bible is a guide for life no matter what society considers legal…. Becoming intoxicated or high, can leave you with some very large regrets. A good portion of youth in America today goes out drinking alcohol on weekends and chasing instant sexual gratification. However, there are consequences. It has led to women getting sexually assaulted. Young girls becoming pregnant. Millions of men and women obtaining sexually transmitted diseases including the AIDS virus. It has also led to automobile accidents where people have been hurt and killed. You do not even have to leave your home to suffer the consequences of insobriety. In 2018, a 48-year-old woman fell down a garbage chute from the 27th story of her Manhattan apartment building. It was determined that she was intoxicated.

The Effects of Mind-Altering Drugs
If Marijuana becomes legal, it is still something to be avoided. It is a mind-altering drug. Its affects motivation, it impairs learning, judgment, and memory. Marijuana has negative short-term effects, long term effects and physical effects. Over time it results in a decline in the quality of your life. Remember Satan comes to steal, kill and destroy.
Marijuana also impacts the ability to concentrate, which hurts

school and work performance. If your concentration is compromised, it will also hinder you from reading and understanding the Bible. Marijuana also causes a lost interest in activities and interferes with relationships. In the Christian realm, this is called serving and fellowship. Hindering knowledge of the word of God and hindering serving God, is the goal of Satan. It is no wonder the Democrat Party is in favor of legalization of marijuana.

My Experiences with People Using Mind-Altering Drugs

People can say what they want, but if you go back to the beginning of the book I said that the end results overt time will prove truth or lies. I have a lifetime of experiences knowing individuals who have used marijuana and other drugs.

I have a close relative who has smoked marijuana for over 30 years. He is now in his mid-fifties. His entire working life, he took jobs that allowed him to have the freedom to smoke marijuana and drink alcohol. He never wanted to work a regular 9 to 5 job with daily responsibilities even though he had a family to support. Today, he speaks erratically and irrationally. He is homeless, and he has no retirement or Social Security. His daughter took him in to care for him, because he can no longer work.

Doing Christian ministry in the inner city, I have seen the effects of drug use on an entire community. I have encountered many individuals whose minds do not function properly from their own drug use or from the drug use of their mother while they were in the womb. The effects are evident within the first few moments that you speak to them.

My wife and I once bought food for a young couple who were living in a tent in the backyard of an abandoned house. They were both in the late twenties and both unemployed. When we brought them the food, we also prayed for them. When I looked down, I saw needle marks all over the young man's arm.

Another young couple in their twenties lived in a rundown house that looked as if it was condemned. The girl had a job, but her boyfriend stayed home all day and smoked marijuana. The girlfriend complained that he was lazy and refused to even attempt to get a job. The young man was in and out of jail all the time and they lived in poverty.

Busy intersections in the city usually had people standing holding signs asking for money. When you looked closely, you could tell from their faces and bodies, drugs had taken a toll on their lives.

I did not mention the drug related violence that took place in the city. Drug addicts robbed people and broke in homes for money. People were killed over drug deals gone bad. Gun shots at night and helicopters flying overhead looking for criminals was a daily occurrence.

An Encounter I will never Forget

There is one encounter with someone addicted to drugs that I will never forget. One Sunday morning, a mother brought her son to the church my wife and I pastored. He was in his early forties. We asked to pray for him, but he refused prayer. He was restless during the entire service. When the service was over, during fellowship, I noticed something was wrong. He acted irrational and said things that were nonsensical. The 12-year old children around him acted more mature and spoke more coherently. It was very uncomfortable.

He never returned to our church. Six months later, we got notice from a friend that he had died from a drug overdose. I learned that his mother fought a lifetime battle trying to help him overcome addiction to drugs. I also learned that he was homeless a great deal of time. My wife and I attended his funeral. His mother who had brought him to our church was distraught. At the funeral, some of his friends spoke. It was obvious that his closest friends (not relatives) were addicted to drugs and that drugs had taken a toll on their lives. They spoke in a nonsensical manner…

This handsome young man's life was prematurely over. He had corrupted his body with drugs and he never fulfilled the call God had on his life.

God Has Set You Apart

God has a plan for your life and Satan also has a plan for your life. God's plan is to set you apart, to do good works for Him and live a life of abundance. Satan's plan to steal, kill and destroy. The choice is up to you. You are not to live according to the lusts of the flesh (the world's standards), but by the Holy Spirit (God's standards). The following scriptures reflect that God intends you to live a holy (sanctified) life and to do good works. To "sanctify" something is to set it apart for special use and to "sanctify" a person is to make them holy.

Before Jesus went to the cross he prayed for the disciples. The Bible says, *"I (Jesus) do not pray that You should take them out of the world, but that You should keep them from the evil one. They are not of the world, just as I am not of the world. Sanctify them by Your truth. Your word is truth. As You sent Me into the world, I also have sent them into the world. And for their sakes I sanctify Myself, that they also may be sanctified by the truth."* (John 17:15-19)

Jesus prayed that the disciples be in the world, but not of it. It means to not live according to the world's sinful values. Jesus prayed the disciples be kept safe from Satan as he sends them out to preach the Gospel and they be made holy by God's truth.

Jesus then prayed for all believers.

The Bible says, *"I (Jesus) do not pray for these alone, but also for those who will believe in Me through their word; that they all may be one, as You, Father, are in Me, and I in You; that they also may be one in Us, that the world may believe that You sent Me. And the glory which You gave Me I have given them, that they may be one just as We are one: I in them, and You in Me; that they may be made perfect in one, and that the world may know that You have sent Me, and have loved them as You have loved Me."* (John 17:20-23)

Jesus prayed for you. He prayed that the world will believe in God through you. If you live a life contrary to the word of God, how are you any different from the world? A drunk preacher going to strip clubs, doing drugs and cheating on his wife is not the example God wants you to set. People are not going to see a holy God by you living like the world.

Workmanship
The Bible says, *"For we are His workmanship, created in Christ Jesus for good works, which God prepared beforehand that we should walk in them."* (Ephesians 2:10)

You are a work of art, created by God. You would not disrespect, destroy or degrade a piece of art by Michelangelo or Davinci. You are greater than that. You are a masterpiece created by God and so you should not degrade yourself or others. You are here on this earth for a purpose. It is not just to sit around, use up resources and the world to revolve around you. There is a calling on your life from God to do His work here on earth.

Crucify the Flesh

The Bible says, *"I have been crucified with Christ; it is no longer I who live, but Christ lives in me; and the life which I now live in the flesh I live by faith in the Son of God, who loved me and gave Himself for me."* (Galatians 2:20)

The Bible says that we are to crucify the flesh and live by faith. This means we are to deny the worldly lusts within us that once ruled over us before we gave our lives to the Lord. Horatius Bonar said, "Denying self is the beginning, the middle, and the end of our course here, as followers of Christ." Worldly lusts can be completely legal such as drinking alcohol, over-eating, being lazy, cursing, getting angry, committing adultery…. However, those behaviors are not Godly, and neither is smoking marijuana, whether it is legal or not.

Sanctification Takes Time

The Bible says, *"Now may the God of peace Himself sanctify you completely; and may your whole spirit, soul, and body be preserved blameless at the coming of our Lord Jesus Christ."* (1 Thessalonians 5:23)

Once you dedicate your life to the Lord, there are many worldly habits that are still part of your flesh. Do not be discouraged as you battle to deny them. With time and as you learn the word of God, you will grow to become more like Christ. That is our goal as a Christian, to become Christ like. When I first gave my life to the Lord, I could not even pray in public. However, in time, I was leading prayer meetings. Billy Graham said, "Being a Christian is more than just an instantaneous conversion; it is like a daily process whereby you grow to be more and more like Christ." It is the will of God for your holiness. We must be obedient to God in all aspects of our lives not just in some. God did not call us to sin, but to holiness.

Good Workers and Bad Workers

"But in a great house there are not only vessels of gold and silver, but also of

wood and clay, some for honor and some for dishonor. Therefore if anyone cleanses himself from the latter, he will be a vessel for honor, sanctified and useful for the Master, prepared for every good work. Flee also youthful lusts; but pursue righteousness, faith, love, peace with those who call on the Lord out of a pure heart." (2 Timothy 2:20-22)

The Bible also tells us that there will be good workers and bad workers in the kingdom of God. If we are to do God's work, we are to live according to God's standards. You will not be useful to God and you will not be honoring Him, by being a bad worker and your work will not last.

Take up the Cross and Follow Jesus

The Bible says, "Then *Jesus said to His disciples, "If anyone desires to come after Me, let him deny himself, and take up his cross, and follow Me. For whoever desires to save his life will lose it, but whoever loses his life for My sake will find it. For what profit is it to a man if he gains the whole world, and loses his own soul? Or what will a man give in exchange for his soul?"* (Matthew 16:24-26)

Anything, that hinders you in doing God's work, is not the will of God. In fact, it is idol worship, because it is placing those things above God in your life. Jesus said, your soul is much more valuable than any profit you can make on this earth, even more valuable than the entire world. I can tell you that people sell their soul for much less than the world. I once encountered a man in his late thirties that was 150 pounds overweight. He struggled to breath and did not walk well. It was obvious that he corrupted his body with bad food and too much food. I tried to witness to him. I asked him if he knew about Jesus. He said, "I know about the Bible, but what you are asking me is to give up my dirty movies and I am not going to do it." This man was selling his soul for pornography. People sell their soul, for all kinds of things. I had friends that worshipped football. Sunday was not a day for going to church and worshipping God, but a day from morning to night of football.

Finally, Paul said this:

"All things are lawful for me, but all things are not helpful. All things are

lawful for me, but I will not be brought under the power of any" (1 Corinthians 6:12)

"I say then: Walk in the Spirit, and you shall not fulfill the lust of the flesh." (Galatians 5:16)

Again, because something is legal, does not mean it is good for you or right in the sight of God. We are to live our lives according to the spirit, not fulfilling the lust of the flesh.

Jesus Cleanses the Temple

There is a famous scripture regarding Jesus cleansing the temple. Jesus cleansed the temple on two different occasions. The first time is in the book of John.

The Bible says, *"Now the Passover of the Jews was at hand, and Jesus went up to Jerusalem. And He found in the temple those who sold oxen and sheep and doves, and the money changers doing business. When He had made a whip of cords, He drove them all out of the temple, with the sheep and the oxen, and poured out the changers' money and overturned the tables. And He (Jesus) said to those who sold doves, "Take these things away! Do not make My Father's house a house of merchandise!"* (John 2:13-16)

God required that people bring animal offerings as a sacrifice for sin to the temple during Passover. It was required by God that you bring your best. There had to be a consequence for your sin. However, pigeons, sheep, and oxen were being sold outside the temple as a business to the Jewish people. After they were purchased, the animals were then given as an offering to God. It was a perversion of the system of worship. The people were not bringing their best, they were not even bringing their own animals. It was lessening the consequences of sin. It is very similar to the scheme of Democrat Party that desires to eliminate the consequences of sin in your life. Also, God's house is a place of worship and those that were selling the animals were using it to make a profit.

Jesus cleansed the temple on a second occasion in the book of Matthew. The Bible says, *"Then Jesus went into the temple of God and drove out all those who bought and sold in the temple, and overturned the tables of the money changers and the seats of those who sold doves. And He said to them, "It is written, 'My house shall be called a house of prayer,' but you have made it a 'den of thieves.' "And He said to them, "It is written, 'My house shall be called a house of prayer,' but you have made it a 'den of thieves."* (Matthew 21:12-13)

Your Body is a Temple

A temple is a place of worship to God. There was corruption occurring in the temple. The misuse and perversion of the temple made Jesus angry. Jesus cleansed the temple because He wanted it to be pure and uncorrupted. He wanted it to be Holy and set apart for God.

The Bible also calls our physical body a temple. It is because we worship God from our bodies and we pray from our bodies. If our bodies are temples, we should attempt to keep them uncorrupted and holy as well. Set apart for God's use. We should not be doing anything to our bodies to harm it. Once again, it is not just mind-altering drugs that we should refrain from, it is anything that harms the body. This includes, cigarettes, alcohol, eating unhealthy foods, eating too much food, laziness, cutting, self-harm, suicide…

Lack of Knowledge of God's Word

The Democrat Party easily leads non-believers astray regarding this issue. However, they also lead Christians astray and it is because of lack of knowledge of the word of God. My wife and I have had people come to our church that support legalization of marijuana. We are to treat are bodies as holy temples. I have heard professional athletes that call themselves Christians support legalization of marijuana. These athletes in the NFL and NBA support legalization of marijuana and call themselves Christian. If you watch an NBA basketball game, it is hard to find a player that does not have a tattoo. It is not just one tattoo it will be their entire upper bodies. What does the Bible say about tatoos?

The Bible says, *"You shall not make any cuttings in your flesh for the dead, nor tattoo any marks on you: I am the Lord."* (Leviticus 19:28)

Your time on earth is not long

Anyone who has lived on this earth past the age of thirty, will tell you that time passes quickly. I look at my own life and I wonder where has the time gone? My parents have passed on and it has been many years now. I miss them dearly! I remember like it was yesterday when I was just a little boy going to the store with them and playing in the backyard. When compared to eternity, your life is just a momentary flash.

Bible says, *"whereas you do not know what will happen tomorrow. For what is your life? It is even a vapor that appears for a little time and then vanishes away."* (James 4:14)

Many pastors have prayed for people on their death bed. There is not a person on the verge of death that has said they wished they spent more time working or chasing selfish desires. People say they wish they had spent more time with their family, wish they had done more for people, expressed their love for their children and for others… In short, they wished they had not spent their lives chasing the foolish things of the flesh, such as mind-altering drugs. Watchman Nee said, "There is nothing more tragic than to come to the end of life and know we have been on the wrong course."

The Bible says, *"See then that you walk circumspectly, not as fools but as wise, redeeming the time, because the days are evil. Therefore do not be unwise, but understand what the will of the Lord is. And do not be drunk with wine, in which is dissipation; but be filled with the Spirit, speaking to one another in psalms and hymns and spiritual songs, singing and making melody in your heart to the Lord, giving thanks always for all things to God the Father in the name of our Lord Jesus Christ"* (Ephesians 5:15-20)

Liberty

V

FREEDOM VERSUS BONDAGE

Satan Appears as an Angel of Light: We the government are here to help you and take care of your needs.

Satan's Goal: Have you become dependent on government instead of God. To replace God in your life and trap you in bondage.

What does the Bible say? *"Do not turn to idols, nor make for yourselves molded gods: I am the Lord your God."* (Leviticus 19:4)

This first chapter sets the stage for the remaining chapters in this section. The Democrat Party, like Satan desires to entrap you in bondage. Their ultimate goal, just as with Satan is to become a god (an idol) to you. It is a false god, because God does not want you trapped in bondage. Democrats accomplish this with an elaborate scheme of providing for needs and wants in the form of government handouts (call them benefits or entitlements) and over a period of time entrapping you in a system of dependency. It is a complicated and deceptive scheme. It is so deceptive that if you were not aware of it, you could fall for their trap…

Satan's Fall

The Bible says that Satan was once called Lucifer in heaven. He was an arch angel. However, Satan became prideful. The book of Isaiah describes how he desired to be like God.

The Bible says, *"For you have said in your heart: I will ascend into heaven, I will exalt my throne above the stars of God; I will also sit on the mount of the congregation On the farthest sides of the north; [14] I will ascend above the heights of the clouds, I will be like the Most High."* (Isaiah 14:13-14)

The Bible says Satan was cast out of heaven for his pride. He wanted to be worshipped like God. It is the reason God hates pride.

The Tactics of Satan

Once cast from heaven, Satan became God's enemy. God desires a relationship with you and Satan wants to destroy you. In the first book of the Old Testament, Satan deceived Eve in the Garden.

The Bible says, *"And the woman said to the serpent, "We may eat the fruit of the trees of the garden; but of the fruit of the tree which is in the midst of the garden, God has said, 'You shall not eat it, nor shall you touch it, lest you die.' "Then the serpent said to the woman, "You will not surely die. For God knows that in the day you eat of it your eyes will be opened, and you will be like God, knowing good and evil." So when the woman saw that the tree was good for food, that it was pleasant to the eyes, and a tree desirable to make one wise, she took of its fruit and ate. She also gave to her husband with her, and he ate. Then the eyes of both of them were opened, and they knew that they were naked; and they sewed fig leaves together and made themselves coverings."* (Genesis 3:2-7)

Satan lied and twisted the word of God tempting Eve. Eve believed Satan, disobeyed God and it led to sin and to the fall of man.

In the First book of the New Testament, Satan lied and twisted the word of God, tempting Jesus.

The Bible says, *"Then Jesus was led up by the Spirit into the wilderness to be tempted by the devil. And when He had fasted forty days and forty nights, afterward He was hungry. Now when the tempter came to Him, he said, "If You are the Son of God, command that these stones become bread." But He answered and said, "It is written, 'Man shall not live by bread alone, but by every word that proceeds from the mouth of God.'" Then the devil took Him up into the holy city, set Him on the pinnacle of the temple, and said to Him, "If You are the Son of God, throw Yourself down. For it is written: 'He shall give His angels charge over you,' and, 'In their hands they shall bear you up, Lest you dash your foot against a stone.'" Jesus said to him, "It is written again, 'You shall not tempt the Lord your God.'" Again, the devil took Him up on an exceedingly high mountain, and showed Him all the kingdoms of the world and their glory. And he said to Him, "All these things I will give You if You will fall down and worship me." Then Jesus said to him, "Away with you, Satan! For it is written, 'You shall worship the Lord your God, and Him only you shall serve.' "Then the devil left Him, and behold, angels came and ministered to Him."* (Matthew 4:1-11)

Jesus did not fall for the lies, deception and tempting of Satan. Jesus knew the word of God and used it to combat Satan. As a result, man was redeemed.

If you look at the tactics of Satan, he lied, twisted the word of God and used temptation. He tempted both Eve and Jesus with the lust of the flesh, the lust of the eyes and the pride of life.

The Bible says, *"For all that is in the world—the lust of the flesh, the lust of the eyes, and the pride of life—is not of the Father but is of the world."* (1 John 2:15)

Satan and Democrats want to Eliminate the Bible in Society
This is very important! Knowing the word of God is the difference between Eve falling for the lies of Satan and Jesus not. Jesus could not be deceived because He knew the word of God. It is the reason Satan and the Democrat Party want to eliminate God and the Bible in society. If you do not know the Bible, you will fall for Satan's lies when they twist the word of God. If Satan lied, twisted the word of God and tempted both Eve and Jesus, he will do the same to you. Satan knows your weaknesses; he will tempt you with the lust of the eyes, the lust of the flesh and pride of life. Satan will lead you into sin and bondage. I said I wanted to give you the belt of truth. You must know the word of God (truth) to fight off the schemes of Satan.

The Bible says, *"And you shall know the truth, and the truth shall make you free."* (John 8:32)

A Corrupt and Perverse Way to get Elected
One of the most corrupt ways you could think of for a political party to win an election would be to just simply buy votes. Hand out cash to people as they go to the voting booths and say, "vote for

me". That is illegal, but when you reclassify that money as government handouts it becomes entirely legal.

Trading government handouts for votes is a corruption of the political system. However, an even greater corruption than that would be to use other people's money or your opponent's money to fund the government handouts in exchange for votes. This is exactly what the Democrat Party does.

However, Satan is never satisfied. To take this corruption to an even more perverse level, would make those government handouts so easily obtainable that people become dependent on the handouts to survive, entrapping them in a system of dependence. Over a period of time, then becoming so dependent on these government handouts, they are used as leverage to their advantage during elections.

Once in bondage and entrapped in these handouts, the Democrat Party will say to those receiving the handouts, "if you vote for them (the opposing party), you will lose your free health care, your food stamps, your free housing, everything, including your freedom." In almost every election you hear the same rhetoric and accusations from the Democrat Party. Their opposition wants to starve children, throw people out on the streets, poison the rivers, kill the elderly… Some recent Democrat Party ads showed Paul Ryan murdering a grandmother in a wheelchair by pushing her off a cliff. A political ad run against George W. Bush showed a pickup truck dragging a black man down a dirt road.

God Supplies your Needs and you are to Trust in Him

Everything in the Democrat Party begins and ends with the idolatry of government. The Democrat Party desires to be a place of refuge for you. A refuge is a place that provides protection. The Democrat Party want you to trust them at all times and in all occasions. However, it is not the purpose of government to supply your needs. The Bible says God is to supply your needs and you are to rely on Him.

The Bible says, *"And my God shall supply all your need according to His riches in glory by Christ Jesus."* (Philippians 4:19)

Also, nowhere in the Bible does it say to trust in government. In fact, "In God we trust" is the official motto of the United States. It comes from the Bible.

The Bible says, *"Trust in Him (God) at all times, you people; Pour out your heart before Him; God is a refuge for us."* (Psalm 62:8)

In the book of Genesis, God spoke to Noah and told him to build an ark. For over 100 years, Noah worked diligently on building the ark. Noah listened to the voice of God and did all that the Lord commanded him. Noah trusted in the Lord and remained faithful. As a result, he and his family were saved from the great flood.

In the book of Exodus, God wanted Moses to lead His people out of bondage and slavery in Egypt. God spoke to Moses and told him, *"to go to Pharaoh, and bring the children of Israel out of Egypt?"* The Bible says then Moses answered, *"But suppose they will not believe me or listen to my voice; suppose they say, 'The Lord has not appeared to you.' "So the Lord said to him, "What is that in your hand?" He (Moses) said, "A rod." And He (God) said, "Cast it on the ground." So he (Moses) cast it on the ground, and it became a serpent; and Moses fled from it. Then the Lord said to Moses, "Reach out your hand and take it by the tail" (and he reached out his hand and caught it, and it became a rod in his hand), "that they may believe that the Lord God of their fathers, the God of Abraham, the God of Isaac, and the God of Jacob, has appeared to you."*

Moses fled from the snake in fear. However, he listened to the voice of God. He faced his fears and grabbed the snake by the tail. Miracles can happen when you trust God. Moses trusted in God and he was able to lead the people out of slavery from Egypt. We are to listen to God and put our faith and trust in Him.

Democrats Mock those that Listen to the Voice of God

The Democrat Party does not want you listening to the voice of God. They want you to listen to anyone, but God. Democrat Al Gore said in 2018, "climate change skeptics should listen to mother nature." He left God out of the equation, putting nature above God. In fact, if you do listen to God, Democrats will mock you. Joy Behar a co-host of the television show 'The View', said regarding Vice President Mike Pence's Christian faith, "talking to Jesus is one thing, but hearing Jesus talk to you could be described as "mental illness."

If we are not to listen to God, who then who are we to listen too?

We could listen to man? As noted in the previous chapters, man and his standards are flawed. Also, a person's intentions for you may not always in your best interest, so advice given to you may be intentionally wrong. As I noted, the Democrat Party intentionally lies and deceives twisting the word of God. If not God and not man, the only one left to listen to would be Satan.

Know the word of God! Horatius Bonar said, "The lie comes sometimes from man, sometimes from Satan, but never from God, for God is not a man that he should lie; never from the works of God when rightly interpreted and understood." Jesus himself says that His followers hear His voice. Jesus said to those who were questioning who He was, *"My sheep hear My voice and I know them, and they follow me."* (John 10:27)

God has a Future and a Hope for You

God always has your best interest in mind. As a parent, you want your children to make good choices, live good lives, have freedom and to prosper. You would not want to hear your little child say, "I hope one day that I live on government handouts trapped in poverty living in public housing." It is quite the opposite. You want your child to have a future and a hope. You give your child guidelines to live by and when they become adults, hope they use the wisdom you gave them and the freedom they enjoy making the right decisions to have an abundant life. This is what God wants for you.

The Bible says, *"For I (God) know the thoughts that I think toward you, says the Lord, thoughts of peace and not of evil, to give you a future and a hope."* (Jeremiah 29:11)

God's thoughts toward us are of peace and to have a future and a hope. He gives us His Word (the Bible) as a guide for life, He speaks to us through the Holy Spirit and through pastors. It is His voice that we should listen to…

The Democrat Party is not for Freedom

The Democrat Party is the party of big government and regulation. It is the reason they always support tax increases and never tax cuts. Ronald Reagan said, "Republicans believe every day is 4th of July, but Democrats believe every day is April 15." Democrats want to control every aspect of your life. They believe in a large centralized federal government in Washington, D.C. taking away decisions and choices of individuals. That is not freedom and it is contrary to what God intends for your life. Democrats believe they know what is better for you than you do yourself. It is one of the reasons Obamacare was such a big deal for the Democrat Party. Instead of you making decisions about your own health, they will, because they know better and desire to control you. You are to bow down to them and not God. It is done to take away your choices and become further in bondage to the Democrat Party. It is all part of their scheme…

Too Much Regulation is Bondage

Once again the Democrat Party aligns with Satan. Over-regulation and removing freedom of choices is bondage. To understand how the Democrat Party twists truth, Democrat President Barack Obama imposed a record number of government regulations (reducing freedoms) and yet Democrats did not consider him a dictator, in fact many believed that he was a modern-day savior. Republican President Donald Trump cut red tape and government regulations (increasing freedoms) and he was called a dictator by Democrats. When you look at states and cities run by the Democrat Party, there is over regulation, cumbersome red tape and overwhelming tax burdens making life difficult for those who desire the freedom to prosper. Winston Churchill said, "If you have ten thousand regulations you destroy all respect for the law." These laws that are out of order, always make things worse.

I remember reading about a city that proposed small water tanks for toilets to save water when you flush the toilet. Sounds good doesn't it? What happened? People flushed twice as much, because the toilets did not provide enough pressure to remove all the waste in the toilet. The result was greater water usage.

In recent years, the liberal run city of Seattle passed a "Head Tax" that required large companies to pay an additional $500 per employee head tax a year. The result was that large companies like Amazon that were looking for a place to open large operations centers passed on opening centers in the city, because it would be too costly. The intended result ended up being detrimental to the city.

There has been new trend, banning plastic straws in restaurants by environmentalists. A restaurant that uses plastic straws can face major fines. However, this presents a problem for those with disabilities. A soggy paper straw increases the chance of choking for certain individuals with disabilities.

Common sense will tell you that imposing and placing massive regulations over everyday life by a large centralized government will lead to failure and restrict freedoms. You cannot have the same laws in Alaska where a resident needs a moose hunting rifle (wild animals) as in New York where there are no moose and bears. In Florida, tourism drives the economy. In Idaho potatoes and farming drive the economy. Every state is different to some degree and cannot be governed with one broad brush.

This is just the tip of the iceberg. They say the United States Tax Code has 5 times as many words as the Bible. The United States has laws and regulations governing every area of society and then overlapping of regulations. Over regulation is not freedom, it is bondage.

Democrat Party Policies are Designed to Make America Fail

The Democrat Party policies are made to fail. As I stated, the Democrat Party does not want you depending on God, so they intentionally institute policies that are designed to fail. The Democrat Party also wants America to fail people. The Democrat Party wants to say, "this freedom you have in America is flawed, capitalism does not work, God is not real! You do not need freedom as it is in America, capitalism or God. You need us! You need socialism! We (the government) will take care of you. If socialism failed in the past, it is because it was not true socialism. Vote for us and we will take care of you."

If you look at the Democrat Party, they want to fundamentally change America. America was founded on freedom from tyranny, separation of powers and giving people the right to vote for its leaders. You must understand that Satan takes what is good and perverts it into something bad. Perversion is the alteration of something from its original course and meaning, or corruption of what was first intended. God gives us love, Satan turn it into lust. God gives us art, Satan turns it into pornography.

Harvard College, the first Ivy League school was established to advance the Christian faith. This is true for the other Ivy League schools. Harvard was named after a Christian minister, Yale was established by clergy to educate Congregational ministers and Princeton's first year of class was taught by a reverend. However, today those institutions have been turned into liberal organizations supporting anti-Christian values. They have been perverted from their original intent.

When Democrat Barack Obama became president, he said, "We are five days away from fundamentally transforming the United States of America." Obama wanted to fundamentally transform America. Obama wanted to pervert America from its original intention.

James Dobson, founder of Focus on the Family, said this, "We must vote, vote, vote to elect leaders who will defend what has been purchased with the blood of patriots who died to protect our liberty. We owe it to the memory of their sacrifice to preserve what they did for us. We must not fritter it away on our watch! If any politician tells you he will 'fundamentally change' this nation, what he means is that he plans to undermine our Constitution and take away our heritage of freedom. Run from him or her!"

God did not make you a robot. God gives you freedom to choose your own path in life. He gives you freedom to choose between good and evil. He gives you the freedom to believe in Him or not. You cannot make someone love you and God wants you to love him voluntarily.

The Bible says, *"I (God) call heaven and earth as witnesses today against you, that I have set before you life and death, blessing and cursing; therefore choose life, that both you and your descendants may live."* (Deuteronomy 30:19)

This freedom that God gives you is freedom designed for His purposes. It is freedom to preach the Gospel, do His will and serve others… You see in many countries, Christianity is outlawed, and you can even go to prison for possessing a Bible. This freedom God gives you is not to do anything that you please. It is not the liberal definition of freedom, which is, if it feels good do it.

The Bible says, *"For you, brethren, have been called to liberty; only do not use liberty as an opportunity for the flesh, but through love serve one another."* (Galatians 5:13)

God is a creator. He created the universe. God created us in His image and God knows you will also create great things if given the chance. He gives you freedom to create. Satan is not a creator, again, he is a perverter. He takes what God creates and perverts it. The founding fathers established America to allow people to have freedom to worship God and to choose their own paths in life. It was not a country established to entrap people into bondage. Milton Freidman said, "The greatest advances of civilization, whether in architecture or painting, in science and literature, in industry or agriculture, have never come from centralized government."

Jesus is freedom and Satan is bondage. You can choose liberty and eternal life by following Jesus, or you can choose bondage and destruction by following Satan. There is no better example than the encounter by the rich young ruler with Jesus. The rich young ruler asked Jesus what he could do to inherit the Kingdom of God?

The Bible says, *"Then Jesus, looking at him, loved him, and said to him, "One thing you lack: Go your way, sell whatever you have and give to the poor, and you will have treasure in heaven; and come, take up the cross, and follow Me." But he was sad at this word, and went away sorrowful, for he had great possessions."* Mark 10:21-22

Jesus told the rich young ruler the truth. Jesus gave him a choice of following the world or not. It was then up to the rich young ruler to decide. Jesus represents freedom.

The Bible says, *"Now the Lord is the Spirit; and where the Spirit of the Lord is, there is liberty."* (2 Corinthians 3:17)

The Bible also says, *"Standfast therefore in the liberty by which Christ has made us free, and do not be entangled again with a yoke of bondage."* (Galatians 5:1)

The next few chapters are in specific order because it follows a scheme (progression) of lies by the Democrat Party. A scheme of bondage with an ultimate objective to become a God (an idol) to people. The idolatry of government is a vicious cycle that is not

Biblical. Just as Moses led the Israelites out of bondage from Egypt
and Jesus came to set you free from the bandage of Satan, God want
you to live in freedom. The Democrat Plan is contrary, and their
scheme of bondage is as follows.

The Idolatry of Government

Identity Politics - Divide people into groups.
Victimization & Blame: Label groups as victims and place blame
on others.
Propose a False Solution: The need for a level playing field and
closing the wealth gap.
Implement a Progressive Tax System: Penalize those they blame.
Wealth Redistribution: Transfer wealth to those identified as
victims.
The Idolatry of Government: Create continual dependence on
government.

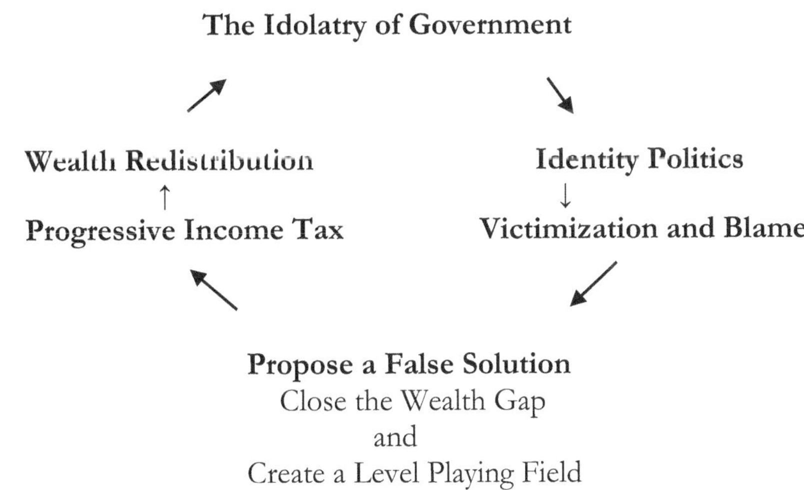

What you must know is that everything that the Democrat Party
promises to do and all they want to become in your life, Jesus already
is!

The Bible says, *"The Spirit of the Lord is upon Me, Because He has anointed Me To preach the gospel to the poor; He has sent Me to heal the brokenhearted, To proclaim liberty to the captives And recovery of sight to the blind, To set at liberty those who are oppressed."* (Luke 4:18)

VI

IDENTITY POLITICS

Satan Appears as an Angel of Light: Divide people into groups to identify needs, wants, some mistreatment or discrimination (real or imagined).

Satan's Goal: Cause division and strife between people.

What does the Bible say?
"There is neither Jew nor Greek, there is neither slave nor free, there is neither male nor female; for you are all one in Christ Jesus." (Galatians 3:28)

"Every kingdom divided against itself is brought to desolation, and a house divided against a house falls." (Luke 11:17)

The first step in the process of the idolatry of government by the Democrat Party is identity politics. Identity politics refers to separating (dividing) people into groups based on needs, wants, some mistreatment or discrimination (real or imagined). It is the scheme of taking a political stance to target specific groups for their votes. For example, to obtain the homosexual vote, the Democrat Party supports gay marriage. To obtain the immigrant vote, they support open borders. The Democrat Party supports abortion to obtain the female vote (unborn babies cannot vote).

You must understand that division is a tactic of Satan. Satan divided heaven causing a great war. He rebelled against God and took one third of the angels with him. If Satan would divide heaven, he will divide earth.

Rush Limbaugh said, "I abhor identity politics because it's separates us. There's no unity. There's no togetherness. It's hopeless, in fact, with identity politics. It's literally hopeless, which I think illustrates the total fraud that is the left-wing agenda, as they state it."

Calvin Coolidge said, "Liberty is not collective, it is personal. All liberty is individual liberty."

To truly understand how corrupt this ideology is, you only need to look at the Democrat Party platform on funding social programs over funding the defense of the country (military). Let me say it again, The Democrat Party supports funding social programs over the military. Their platform is based on the sheer number of possible votes. It is not based on the Constitution or what is best for America. It is based on what is in the best interest of the Democrat Party. There are approximately 1.2 million U.S. military personnel and another 800,000 in reserves. If you add military spouses, you are looking at 4 million possible military voters. That is if every person in the military voted against the Democrat Party. However, if the US population is 325 million and 10% are considered in poverty, that translates to 32 million possible voters. It is a position solely based on obtaining the most possible votes. This position is contrary to the United States Constitution and what is intended in the formation of America. Government's primary responsibility is national defense and the preservation of the country.

Abraham Lincoln said, "The legitimate object of government is to do for a community of people whatever they need to have done, but cannot do at all, or cannot so well do, for themselves in their separate and individual capacities."

William F. Buckley, Jr. said, "Liberals, it has been said, are generous with other people's money, except when it comes to questions of national survival when they prefer to be generous with other people's freedom and security."

It is Compassionate to Help Others
I would say helping those in need is Biblical. Government does have safety nets in place such as unemployment that pays individuals

who have lost their job for a limited time. However, to provide endless government handouts to healthy and strong individuals that have no impairments to work, is not compassionate and it is not Biblical.

Helping people is not the ultimate objective of the Democrat Party. As I stated, it is the idolatry of government. It is trapping people in the bondage of endless government handouts to trade money for votes. However, to do this, the Democrat Party first must separate people into groups to determine how to trade their handouts for votes.

Love your Neighbor as Yourself

What does the Bible say about how to treat others? This is a scripture that many know, even those that do not go to church. What is interesting is that not only does this scripture address how to treat others (identity politics), it also addresses the idolatry of government.

The Bible says, *"And you shall love the Lord your God with all your heart, with all your soul, with all your mind, and with all your strength.' This is the first commandment. And the second, like it, is this: 'You shall love your neighbor as yourself.' There is no other commandment greater than these."* (Mark 12:30-31)

The Bible says the fist commandment is that that we are to love God (not government) will our hearts, souls and minds. God comes first. We are to place nothing above God in our lives. Next, we are to love our neighbors (not divide and separate) as ourselves. God commands that we are to treat people as we wish to be treated. The Democrat Party making themselves an idol to people and dividing people is in direct contrast to the word of God.

In the book of James, it tells us that we shall love our neighbor as ourselves, but it also says that if we show partiality between people it is a sin.

The Bible says, *"If you really fulfill the royal law according to the Scripture, "You shall love your neighbor as yourself," you do well; but if you show partiality, you commit sin, and are convicted by the law as transgressors." (James 2:8-9)*

The Bible is clear, we are to love others as we love ourselves and if

we show partiality it is a sin. This is exactly what the Democrat Party
is doing when they engage in identity politics. They are dividing
people and showing partiality. It is contradictory to the word of God

A New Commandment

Before Jesus went to the cross, He gave us a new commandment
regarding love. As a Christian, you are called to a very high standard
of love. The Bible is a love story. It is God's love for you. God gave
His son to you as a gift to redeem you from sin. The only thing God
ever gets for all He has done and given is a relationship with you. All
God desires is a relationship with you! The earthly ministry of Jesus
was all about love. He came to redeem us all from the curse of sin.
Jesus was God in the flesh and He was love in the flesh.

The Bible says, *"A new commandment I (Jesus) give to you, that you love
one another; as I have loved you, that you also love one another.   By this all will
know that you are My disciples, if you have love for one another."* (John 13:34-
35)

Jesus said that you are to love others as He loved. His love for you
was unconditional and was so great that He came to this Earth was
scourged and crucified for you even though He committed no sin.
No matter how great the crime or sin, Jesus paid the price for you.
He gave his life for every sinner, no matter the race or gender even
though they did not deserve such an act. This includes thieves,
rapists, child molesters and murderers. This is an incredible love and
Jesus commanded us to love others as He loved. God does not show
partiality between people.

The Bible says, *"There is neither Jew nor Greek, there is neither slave nor
free, there is neither male nor female; for you are all one in Christ Jesus."*
(Galatians 3:28)

According to God, no one is Irredeemable

During the 2016 election, Hillary Clinton (Democrat) called
Donald Trump (Republican) supporters "deplorables", but what
seemed to be missed is that she also called them "irredeemable". The
nominee for Democrat Party for President of the United States
claimed that people were "irredeemable". The definition of

irredeemable is being beyond remedy. It means that they can never be fixed. According to God, there is no one that is irredeemable.

In the Book of Acts, Saul of Tarsus, persecuted, tortured and murdered Christians. However, one day on the road to Damascus he had an encounter with Jesus. After that encounter, Saul dedicated his life to Jesus and became the Apostle Paul. Once a murderer of Christians, Paul became the greatest evangelist that ever lived and wrote two thirds of the New Testament. Hillary was wrong. Anyone can be redeemed (saved) even murderers once they have an encounter and turn their life over to Jesus.

We are Ambassadors for Christ

When I first started attending church, a young couple wanted to be greeters. They were not married and living together, which is not Biblical. The church told them that they would have to be married to be greeters. The young couple did not understand the word of God, they wanted to live in sin and represent the church. K.P. Yohannan said, "Jesus' reason for taking 12 men to be His disciples was to teach them—through His example and the events of life—how to live like Him and do what He did." If you are a Christian, you are to adhere to the word of God and not oppose it. In fact, the Bible tells us that we are to become like Jesus.

The Bible says, *"He who says he abides in Him (Jesus) ought himself also to walk just as He walked."* (1 John 2:6)

The owner of a company wants the workers to represent the organization a certain way. To dress, speak, act appropriately and represent the values of the company. Imagine you own company and your worker is going on television, dressed poorly, using foul language and saying things that are contrary to the company... I think you would fire them.

Christians are called to walk like Jesus. We are His ambassadors on this earth. It always disturbs me when I see people proclaiming to be Christians actively opposing the word of God. Imagine how God feels? God wants us representing His kingdom in a Godly manner and consistent with His word.

The Bible says, *"Now then, we are ambassadors for Christ, as though God were pleading through us: we implore you on Christ's behalf, be reconciled to God."* (2 Corinthians 5:20)

In the matter of identity politics, the Bible is clear, God is against treating people differently. The Bible says, *"love your neighbor"*, *"love one another"* and if we *"show partiality"* it is a sin. Even greater than that, we are to love people as Jesus loved. If you are to call yourself a Christian, you must represent God and participating in identity politics is contrary to the word of God. Love does not divide; it brings people together. The Bible warns you of the ultimate objective of the Democrat Party in the first step of their divisive scheme.

The Bible says, *"Every kingdom divided against itself is brought to desolation, and a house divided against a house falls."* (Luke 11:17)

The Hypocrisy of Democrats

Martin Luther King Jr. was an icon and hero to the Democrat Party and to blacks in America. One of his greatest speeches, "I Have a Dream" contains one of his most cited quotes which is, "I look to a day when people will not be judged by the color of their skin, but by the content of their character." That quote means we are not to judge people by appearance, but by their character. It is based in scripture. Today close to 1,000 streets in America are named after Martin Luther King Jr., predominately in black neighborhoods. These neighborhoods are run by politicians in the Democrat Party and the people that reside in them vote over 90% with the Democrat Party. Yet it is the Democrat Party that survives by identity politics by dividing people on everything except the content of their character.

Why do Some People get away with Doing Bad Things?

Many pose the question, "If there is a just God, why do people who do bad things, get away with it?" I will give you the answer. If God punished you immediately for your sins, you would not live past the age of 10 and no one on earth would live past the age of 18. God is patient and gives you time to change and turn from sin. I can tell you that in my youth I did many things that I am not proud of and were not pleasing to God. I drank alcohol to excess and had sex outside of marriage. However, when I got saved and dedicated my life to Jesus, I planted a church, I preached the Gospel through websites and then wrote this book. God will give you time. He desires a relationship with you, but that time is on His schedule. Accept Jesus as your Lord and Savior before it is too late.

The Love Test

I will end this chapter by giving you the "Love Test". There is a television show called, "Love Island" where male and female participants are thrown together on a tropical paradise to see what relationships develop. The show really should be called "Lust Island". Lust is defined as very strong sexual desire. That show is not about and has nothing to do with love.

I came up with, The Love Test" when I was writing a sermon. The greatest description of love was written by Paul in the New Testament. If you are a Christian, you know this scripture.

The Bible says, *"Love suffers long and is kind; love does not envy; love does not parade itself, is not puffed up; does not behave rudely, does not seek its own, is not provoked, thinks no evil; does not rejoice in iniquity, but rejoices in the truth; bears all things, believes all things, hopes all things, endures all things."* (1 Corinthians 13:4-7)

The Bible says that Jesus is love. If you substitute Jesus for the word love in that scripture, He holds up…. It says, Jesus suffers long *and* is kind; Jesus does not envy; Jesus does not parade Himself, is not puffed up; does not behave rudely, does not seek His own, is not provoked, thinks no evil; does not rejoice in iniquity, but rejoices in the truth; bears all things, believes all things, hopes all things, endures all things. Jesus holds up to the "Love Test".

If you substitute the Democrat Party in place of love, when it comes to their platform of identity politics, it fails completely! When you divide it is not long suffering, or kind, it is envy, it parades itself, it is rude and seeks its own…. I would ask you to substitute your name in place of the word love and see how you hold up. When you do this, you will see the areas that you need to improve in loving others to become more like Jesus.

VII

VICTIMIZATION AND BLAME

Satan Appears as an Angel of Light: Do not feel bad about your circumstances, whatever they may be. Your situation and troubles are not of your own making. You are not to blame, because you are a victim!

Satan's Goal: Cause division and strife between people.

What does the Bible say? *"Now I urge you, brethren, note those who cause divisions and offenses, contrary to the doctrine which you learned, and avoid them. For those who are such do not serve our Lord Jesus Christ, but their own belly, and by smooth words and flattering speech deceive the hearts of the simple."* (Romans 16:17-18)

Once the Democrat Party divides people into groups, next comes victimization and blame. They make victims of the groups of people. The definition of victim is one that is injured, harmed or tricked under various conditions. They Democrat Party then blames other groups of people that they determine as the privileged in society for the plight of those they have determined are victims. The grievances and blame is done with the intent to cause division and strife between people. The definition of grievance is a real or imagined wrong, cause for complaint or unfair treatment.

Examples of identity politics, victimization and blame:

<u>**Identity Politics**</u>   <u>**Victim**</u>   <u>**Blame**</u>

Homosexuals are denied gay marriage by Christians.
The poor are given an unfair playing field by the wealthy.
Minorities are discriminated against by the majority.
The environment is being destroyed by large corporations.

White Privilege

A big movement began in 2018 by liberals and the Democrat Party called "White Privilege". It is basically societal privilege for being white. It is a way to blame an entire race of people because of any individual failure of a person of color. It means because you are white, you are to blame, because others have made mistakes or failed. It is a way to remove the personal responsibility of a person's own decisions and actions in life.

The Bible says, *"Do not be deceived, God is not mocked; for whatever a man sows, that he will also reap. For he who sows to his flesh will of the flesh reap corruption, but he who sows to the Spirit will of the Spirit reap everlasting life."* (Galatians 6:7-8)

This scripture means that actions have consequences. The things you do in life matter. You cannot plant weeds and expect to grow roses. You cannot steal, do drugs or commit murder and expect not to have troubles.

When I helped pastor a church in Pine Hills, Florida which was an impoverished city where the minorities in America were a majority, drugs were an easy way to make money. Most young men were living contradictory to the word of God. In that city, you were not considered "cool" unless you had spent time in jail. In fact, it was common place for young men to have been arrested and spent time in jail. One young man told me, he preferred jail to living in his house with his family, because he had his own bed, had food and electricity. He was living with his mother in a 3-bedroom house with 12 family members including his older brothers, his sister and her children…

This young man was 24 and had been arrested numerous times. He told me that the police stopped him on one occasion for jaywalking in the middle of the day. When they arrested him, he had the drug "Molly" in his pocket. He was angry and felt targeted by the police. I told him, "the police are trying to keep the community safe and families do not want drugs in their neighborhoods". I said, "there are law abiding people trying to raise a family in this community and you are concerned that the police are going to arrest you and take your drugs away." The last time I saw him, he had violated his probation and was facing nine months in jail. The truth, if there was blame, it was not on the white race, it was on the young man's father for abandoning the family and on the young man himself for getting, stealing and dealing drugs.

What Democrats and liberals will not say is that if you drive two miles, (east or west) from this community of Pine Hills there were four huge shopping centers with clothing stores, restaurants, mobile phone stores, shoe stores, discount stores.... Along the way to those shopping centers were hotels, auto shops, grocery stores, more restaurants... Four miles away was Universal Studios, a community college, a Super Walmart and more restaurants all providing hundreds of job opportunities.

Despite all this opportunity, no one in the young man's house worked or went to school. This young man's entire family was on government handouts. It was a culture of victimization, blame and failure. This young man represented many in his community. Again, it is not his fault that he was raised with no father. However, let's look the events in his life and what the Bible says about those events....

He dropped out of school.
"How much better to get wisdom than gold! And to get understanding is to be chosen rather than silver." (Proverbs 16:16)

"Take firm hold of instruction, do not let go; Keep her, for she is your life." (Proverbs 4:13)

He committed robbery, was arrested and spent time in jail.
"You shall not steal." (Exodus 20:15)

He was arrested for possession of drugs.
"Be sober-minded; be watchful. Your adversary the devil prowls around like a roaring lion, seeking someone to devour." (1 Peter 5:8)

He was arrested for selling drugs.
"If anyone causes one of these little ones—those who believe in me— to stumble, it would be better for them to have a large millstone hung around their neck and to be drowned in the depths of the sea." (Matthew 18:6)

He fathered a child out of wedlock.
"Flee sexual immorality. Every sin that a man does is outside the body, but he who commits sexual immorality sins against his own body." (1 Corinthians 6:18)

He was not working to support the mother and child.
"But if anyone does not provide for his own, and especially for those of his household, he has denied the faith and is worse than an unbeliever." (1 Timothy 5:8)

When you live contrary to the word of God, you are living in accordance with Satan, which brings destruction. Pretty much everything the young man was doing in life was not Biblical. The result of his choices and actions was poverty, homelessness and jail. He was reaping what he was sowing.

This young man, dropped out of school, was arrested for stealing, arrested for possession of drugs, arrested for dealing drugs, fathered a child out of wedlock, was not working to support the mother or child and the Democrat Party is going to point the finger at me and blame me. The Democrat Party is placing judgement on me by blaming me for the plight of individuals who are voting for them and living according to what they are teaching.

This is hypocrisy on the level of the Pharisees because it is the Democrat Party that says you should not blame an entire race for the actions of some. Democrats say that because a certain race commits a high percentage of crimes that you should not judge an entire race based on those statistics. However, it is the Democrat Party that uses the scheme of victimization and blame, which points the finger at entire races of people for individual failures.

When President Barack Obama (Democrat) became president, years into his office he was still blaming President Bush (Republican) for his failures. In 2012, four years into his presidency, Obama said, "We've made sure to do everything we can to dig ourselves out of this incredible hole that I inherited." Can you imagine a football or baseball coach his team's poor performance on a coach from 4 years earlier?

What does the Bible say about Blaming Others?

The Bible says, *"therefore you are inexcusable, O man, whoever you are who judge, for in whatever you judge another you condemn yourself; for you who judge practice the same things. But we know that the judgment of God is according to truth against those who practice such things. And do you think this, O man, you who judge those practicing such things, and doing the same, that you will escape the judgment of God? Or do you despise the riches of His goodness, forbearance, and longsuffering, not knowing that the goodness of God leads you to repentance? But in accordance with your hardness and your impenitent heart you are treasuring up for yourself wrath in the day of wrath and revelation of the righteous judgment of God, who "will render to each one according to his deeds": eternal life to those who by patient continuance in doing good seek for glory, honor, and immortality; but to those who are self-seeking and do not obey the truth, but obey unrighteousness—indignation and wrath, tribulation and anguish, on every soul of man who does evil, of the Jew first and also of the Greek; but glory, honor, and peace to everyone who works what is good, to the Jew first and also to the Greek. For there is no partiality with God."* (Romans 2:1-11)

The Bible says, those who are judging are condemning themselves, they are doing what they are blaming others for. The Bible says they are storing up punishment for themselves for not changing and for keeping their scheme. They are following evil and not good. God knows everything, and you will be judged righteously by God, because He shows no partiality.

The Democrat Party Speaks Failure and Death

As I noted the Democrat Party intentionally institutes policies that fail They want you to fail in order that you depend on them. As a result, their platform is a message of failure. To create victims and blame others, says that you cannot make it on your own. The Democrat Party does not speak life, they speak death over people. Words are powerful. When I would speak to the young men in the community in Pine Hills, FL, many had a victim mentality. They believed the lies of the Democrat Party and fell into their traps… Before I found the Lord, I read many books in my quest for success in the business world. The quotes were true and helped me as I pursued my goals. These truths are in exact opposition to the Democrat Party message of victimization…

Vince Lombardi said, "The difference between a successful person and others is not a lack of strength, not a lack of knowledge, but rather a lack of will."

John Wooden said, "Don't let what you cannot do interfere with what you can do."

Napoleon Hill said, "More gold has been mined from the thoughts of men than has been taken from the earth."

Brian Tracey said, "Successful people are simply those with successful habits."

Norman Vincent Peale said, "Never talk defeat. Use words like hope, belief, faith, victory."

Again, once I dedicated myself to the Lord, I learned all quotes reflecting truth have root in the Bible….

The Bible says:

"Death and life are in the power of the tongue, And those who love it will eat its fruit." (Proverbs 18:21)

"He who would love life And see good days, Let him [refrain his tongue from evil, And his lips from speaking deceit." (1 Peter 3:10)

"Let no corrupt word proceed out of your mouth, but what is good for necessary edification, that it may impart grace to the hearers." (Ephesians 4:29)

"I can do all things through Christ who strengthens me." (Philippians 4:13)

Democrats Ridicule Living Biblically
The Democrat Party is so intent on destroying with their words, that if you try and live a Biblical life, such as getting an education and

working hard they will shame, ridicule and destroy your reputation. Their desire is to keep you trapped in bondage. The young man in Pine Hills, should have got an education, worked hard, not had children until he was married and got himself a good job. However, if you do this, you will be mocked by the Democrat Party.

Democrat Rep. Bennie Thompson of Mississippi in an interview called conservative Supreme Court Justice Clarence Thomas an "Uncle Tom." An Uncle Tom is a derogatory term used by Democrats to put people down who think outside of the Democrat Party platform. Clarence Thomas was educated at Holy Cross College and at Yale Law School. He was appointed an Assistant Attorney General in Missouri and eventually became an associate justice on the United States Supreme Court.

Condoleezza Rice was called an "Aunt Jemima" by liberals. Miss Rice was awarded a B.A., cum laude, in political science by the University of Denver. She then obtained a master's degree in political science from the University of Notre Dame. She also earned a PHD in Political Science. She went on to become Secretary of State under George W. Bush. Four Star General Colin Powell was also called an Uncle Tom by Democrats. Powell was born in Harlem, New York to Jamaican immigrant parents. He joined the military and with hard work and dedication eventually rose to the rank of general. Powell served as Secretary of State under Republican President Bush.

Republican presidential candidate Herman Cain was called a "Modern Day Uncle Tom" and told he "acted like Uncle Remus." Herman Cain's mother was a cleaning woman. Cain received a master of science in computer science from Purdue University. He worked as a ballistics analyst for the U.S. Department of the Navy as a civilian. In 1977, he joined Pillsbury and became director of business analysis in its restaurant and foods group. Eventually, he became president and CEO of Godfather's Pizza.

Republican Presidential candidate Dr. Ben Carson was called by actor Marlon Wayans a "sellout" and an embarrassment to black Americans. Carson graduated with honors from Southwestern University. While there he was also a senior commander in the school's ROTC program. He earned a full scholarship to Yale and graduated with a B.A. degree in psychology. Carson then enrolled in the School of Medicine at the University of Michigan. He became director of pediatric neurosurgery at Johns Hopkins at the age of 33.

These individuals should be looked at as a role models in the black community.   A role model is person who serves as an example of values, attitudes and behaviors. A role model is someone who other individuals aspire to be like. However, this is not the case to those in the Democrat Party and liberals. Some of these individuals have been banned from speaking on liberal college campuses and they are mocked and ridiculed. What does the Bible say about ridiculing others?

The Bible says, *"Let nothing be done through selfish ambition or conceit, but in lowliness of mind let each esteem others better than himself."* (Philippians 2:3-4)

Democrat Role Models do not Reflect Biblical Values
In 2017, Michelle Obama called the singer Beyonce, "a role model for us all". In 2016, Beyonce performed at the Super Bowl half-time show aired across the world. Her performance carried an anti-police message. Sheriffs and police said that Beyoncé was inciting bad behavior and "endangering law enforcement" with her performance. A former Democrat First Lady of the United Sates claims that someone showcasing anti-police messages that incite bad behavior and endanger law enforcement is a role model to all of us.

Beyonce is a very talented singer. There are tens of millions of minorities in America, but there are very few who make it to her level in the entertainment industry. Wouldn't it be better served to make role models out of those that received an education, worked hard and became successful business owners, teachers, lawyers and doctors?

The Bible says to Avoid Division and Strife
Dale Carnegie, said, "The only way to get the best of an argument is to avoid it." It is a quote founded in scripture. What does the Bible say about divisiveness?

The Bible says, *"Now I urge you, brethren, note those who cause divisions and offenses, contrary to the doctrine which you learned, and avoid them. For those who are such do not serve our Lord Jesus Christ, but their own belly, and by smooth words and flattering speech deceive the hearts of the simple."* (Romans 16:17-18)

The Bible says to avoid divisive people, because they do not serve Jesus. They are only serving themselves. They use smooth words to deceive the hearts of the simple. The Democrat Party is intentionally creating divisiveness using fraudulent arguments to deceive people. The Democrat Party once again is doing what the Bible urges you not to do…

God Desires Peace

God loves you! He wants everyone to live in harmony and peace with one another. God is our Father in Heaven. As a parent, how would you feel if your children did not get along? How would you feel if they were fighting with each other, instead of helping each other? It would hurt. Even worse, what if your children were trying to destroy each other? What if their conflict was so great that that your children were enemies and not friends? It would probably destroy you. You want peace and harmony in your family, you want your children to get along and to help each other and so does God.

The Bible says, *"Be of the same mind toward one another. Do not set your mind on high things, but associate with the humble. Do not be wise in your own opinion. Repay no one evil for evil. Have regard for good things in the sight of all men. If it is possible, as much as depends on you, live peaceably with all men."* (Romans 12:16-18)

The Bible says that we are to think highly of our own opinion, not to repay evil and to live in peace with each other. The Democrat Party's scheme of dividing people and then creating victims and blaming is contrary to scripture.

Beware of False Prophets

The Democrat Party in America has a monopoly on the black vote. I gave the example earlier of the young man in Pine Hills, Florida living a life contrary to the word of God. His life was in chaos and he blamed others for his troubles. In that city, the Democrat Party runs unopposed. Republicans do not even attempt to run for election in that district. The Democrat Party has convinced the minority population in that city and many cities like it that their predicament is not of their own making and someone else is to blame. The city is in shambles, with garbage, crime, drugs and poverty everywhere.

There have been three major black leaders of the black community over the last 40 years in America (Al Sharpton, Jesse Jackson and Barack Obama). All are Democrats. Amazing that two of the three claim the title of Reverend and yet everything they stand for is not Biblical. How can a someone with the title reverend support division, gay marriage and abortion? The Bible warns about leaders like these that do more harm than good…

The Bible says, *"Beware of false prophets, who come to you in sheep's clothing, but inwardly they are ravenous wolves. You will know them by their fruits. Do men gather grapes from thornbushes or figs from thistles? Even so, every good tree bears good fruit, but a bad tree bears bad fruit. A good tree cannot bear bad fruit, nor can a bad tree bear good fruit. Every tree that does not bear good fruit is cut down and thrown into the fire. Therefore by their fruits you will know them."* (Matthew 7:15-20)

VIII

PROPOSE A FALSE SOULTION
CREATE A LEVEL PLAYING FIELD AND CLOSE THE INEQUALITY GAP BETWEEN THE RICH AND POOR

Satan Appears as an Angel of Light: We, the government, are going to eliminate mistreatment, poverty, injustice and discrimination. We are going to create a level playing field, close the gap between the rich and poor, and make society fair for everyone.

Satan's Goal: Turn division into jealousy and anger, which leads to violence.

What does the Bible say? *"You shall not covet your neighbor's wife; and you shall not desire your neighbor's house, his field, his male servant, his female servant, his ox, his donkey, or anything that is your neighbor's."* (Deuteronomy 5:21)

Once the Democrat Party divides people into groups using identity politics, labels groups as victims placing blame on others, they next propose that the victimization must be resolved. It is done with the promise to eliminate mistreatment, injustice and discrimination. Their promise is to create a level playing field for all and close the gap between the rich and poor. Closing the gap between rich and poor is self-explanatory. The phrase "level the playing field" means, that everyone in society has an equal chance. It is a completely fraudulent argument. It also is very dangerous, because it creates jealousy, coveting and anger...

Former Democrat President Obama said this, "I believe this is the defining challenge of our time: Making sure our economy works for every working American. It's why I ran for President. But this increasing inequality is most pronounced in our country, and it challenges the very essence of who we are as a people."

Democrat Vermont Senator Bernie Sanders said this, "The issue of wealth and income inequality is the great moral issue of our time, it is the great economic issue of our time, and it is the great political issue of our time."

Democrat Senator Elizabeth Warren said, I've spent my career fighting to level the playing field for working families in America."

The solution to inequality and mistreatment, by creating economic fairness and a level playing field by the Democrat Party is always linked to money. The reason is that when you are not living for God, you live according to the world and the master of the world is money. Billy Graham said, "There is nothing wrong with men possessing riches. The wrong comes when riches possess men."

The Bible says, *"No one can serve two masters; for either he will hate the one and love the other, or else he will be loyal to the one and despise the other. You cannot serve God and mammon."* (Matthew 6:24)

The word mammon means, money, wealth, and material possessions. When the victimization label is placed on a group by the Democrat Party, the solution is always monetary. Example: To resolve global warming that Democrats say is caused by large wealthy developed countries, money (a tax) must be paid to the poor underdeveloped countries (victims).

Closing the Wealth Gap is a Fraudulent Argument
Solving inequality between people sounds good doesn't it? It is not… The claim of closing the wealth gap, leveling the playing field and making society fairer for everyone is a fraudulent, deceptive resolution to a fraudulent premise that all people need to be equal in life. Let me just say, do you know what is fair in society? It is allowing people to earn and keep what they work hard for. Taking from

someone that works hard and giving to someone else is the definition of unfair.

Every person was born with different abilities and talents such as singing, writing, teaching, public speaking, math, science, physics, mechanics or even physical abilities and attributes. Some people love to write, others love to calculate math. Some people are very motivated, some people are lethargic. I love math and I have very little artistic ability. Not only are people gifted differently, people change over time. I was strong, athletic and very energetic when I was young. Today, I do not have as much energy, I am not athletic, and I am physically much weaker.

A person that loves to build and wants to become an architect must sacrifice, study hard and pay for extensive schooling. When you design structures, they need to be engineered properly so they are safe. It takes great calculation to be an architect. An architect deserves the fruits of their labor for sacrificing, getting and education, working hard and taking the risk of building structures. Some of the deadliest man-made disasters were the result of engineering failures. In 1975, the failure of the Banqiao Reservoir Dam in China caused an estimated 171,000 deaths and 11 million more people displaced. It was due to engineering failure.

It would be fallacy and dangerous to pay an architect $10 per hour, the same as an 18-year-old that takes orders at a fast food restaurant. If both were paid the same wage, why would anyone want to become an architect? It would be wiser to flip hamburgers, because you would make the same income without having to pay for schooling, sacrifice, and have the stress and liability of designing a building that could collapse and kill innocent people. It would also be foolish to pay an 18-year-old the same as an architect, because the cost of a hamburger would be about $30. The restaurant would go out of business very quickly. If someone wants to work to become a doctor, so be it. If someone wants to sit on the beach all day, surf the waves and work at a restaurant at night, so be it... Let that person earn the fruits of their labor. Clarence Thomas said, "Government cannot make us equal; it can only recognize, respect, and protect us as equal before the law."

Appearances can be Deceiving

There is another problem with the Democrat scheme of leveling the playing field. Appearances can be deceiving. There are people that make a lot of money, that live in nice houses, wear expensive suits and drive nice cars, but live with under the pressure of mountains of debt. They appear to live extravagant lives, but it is not reality. I once knew a truck driver, who made $70,000 a year. He lived in a big house and drove a new Mercedes Benz. From the outside, people would drive by and say, "that guy is doing great!" On the inside, he was dying. He would tell me that he was under "great stress." His back was hurting, and he was on the verge of losing everything if he took time off from work. It all looked great, but it was a mirage….

Taking away Freedom

Let's say that every person in America, was given the same large salary, the same large house, an expensive car and the same amount of money for food and clothing each month. There would still be a huge gap in the way people lived. Some people are savers and some people are spenders. Some people eat at Capital Grille, while others go to Golden Corral. Some people buy expensive gluten free healthy foods, while others eat hot dogs. Some people look for deals using coupons and others do not. Some people buy clothes at Saks Fifth Avenue and others shop at Walmart. Over a period of time, how you spend your money makes a difference in your bank account. I am going to give you the story of two people that are real...

I have a relative that worked and lived a modest life. He earned a decent wage, but he never spent foolishly. He lived in a modest house, drove a modest car and took modest vacations. You go in his house and he had modest furniture. He also invested his money. Over thirty years, he had saved a good-sized amount of money in a retirement account. As a result, he retired early. He then sold his house and bought a large beautiful home in a very nice city by the beach.

I have another relative that earns more than the relative I just described above. However, this relative spends every penny that he earns. He drives a Cadillac, buys $100 dress shirts, takes trips all over the world, believes that his value comes from the name brand of the clothes he puts on his back. You go in his home, he has a $3,000 couch and $1,000 desk. He has always lived month to month, puts no money in a retirement account. His credit is bad from not paying on credit cards and he does not even own a house.

This is one example. However, after helping to pastor a church in the inner city, I have seen spending habits that include, alcohol, cigarettes, drugs and strip clubs… You can take two people give them the same income and same house payment, however, the money in their bank account at the end of the month will be different. The person spending money recklessly will have far less than a person that does not. Multiply that by years and their bank accounts will not be equal. The Democrat Party solution to this problem would be in time, take from the person that lived wisely and give it to the person who lived recklessly. They punish success and reward failure.

To really illustrate my point and how fraudulent the Democrat Party argument is, I am going to take this to an extreme level. What if there was a way to legislate income, housing, spending on clothes and food for people? What if a married couple has children and another married couple has no children. Is government going to legislate how much to spend on each child every month? Are they going to legislate how many children that you can have? What if a person's car breaks down because they are not responsible and fail to change the oil? How do you legislate and control irresponsibility? If a person runs their air-conditioning at 72 and another at 78, there will be a difference in electric bills each month. If one family likes to take long showers or baths, the water bill will be higher than that of another family of a married couple with no children that only take showers. Is government going to monitor and legislate every aspect of your life including how long the length of your showers and the temperature you set the thermostat?

How do you solve this wealth gap over time? It is not possible, because everyone is different. People's tastes, desires and spending habits are different. There are celebrities that have made more money in one year than I will ever make in my lifetime but have filed bankruptcy because of their spending habits. Unless the Democrat Party wants to create laws governing every detail and aspect of life, their solution to leveling the playing field is fraudulent.

The Greatness of America and Capitalism
I want to touch on the greatness of America and capitalism. Before America and capitalism, through the thousands of years of

history of civilization, it was only the rich that was privileged enough to have entertainment, servants to their wash clothes, nice homes, abundant food to eat, transportation and so on…. If you are wealthy living anywhere in the world today the same is true. The wealthy can afford these things. The wealthy can buy an expensive television, drive a nice car, have servants and live in a nice house and have entertainment. However, that is not the case, if you are poor in a third world country. The poor in third world countries do not enjoy such things. What makes capitalism great is that even the poor in America have access to entertainment, transportation, washing machines and they can even own property. It may not be to the extravagance of the wealthy, but it is obtainable. Capitalism allows for you to buy a million-dollar home or a $30,000 home. It allows you to buy a Rolls Royce or a Ford. You can buy a plasma television or get an inexpensive television. America allows everyone to have the same things, just at different qualities…

Hypocrisy by Democrats and Liberals
There is hypocrisy as always with every Democrat Party position and it is the same with creating a level playing field and reducing the wealth gap between the rich and poor. A millionaire may seem rich to a person earning $50,000 a year, but a person earning $50,000 a year is rich compared to someone earning minimum wage. A person earning minimum wage is very well off compared to a homeless person. A homeless person in America is well off compared to a person in poverty in a third world country. If the Democrats are going to support taking from someone earning $50,000 to give to another earning minimum wage to reduce the wealth gap, why not take from someone earning minimum wage and give to those who are homeless? I have yet to hear anyone in the Democrat Party support redistributing even $1 from someone earning minimum wage to the homeless.

Democrat Policies Create Jealousy Which Leads to Anger
Dividing people, victimizing, blaming and proposing a solution that continually fails only leads down a path to jealousy. It is consistent with the Democrat Party aligning with Satan against God. Jealousy in the Bible is a demon spirit. Jealousy is feeling resentment because of another's success or advantage. The Democrat Party tells

you that you are a victim and it is not your fault. Their solutions fail, because they are meant to fail, so they continually place blame while never recognizing any accountability or personal responsibility of those they claim are victims. Over time those that the Democrat Party claim are victims feel wronged, because their solutions do not work. As a result, jealousy, resentment and anger are born. This is the Democrat scheme, because jealousy leads to resentment, which leads to anger and anger motivates people to act.

The Race Summit

When Democrat Barrack Obama first became president, there was a national discussion relating to a black man who was arrested outside of his house in a wealthy neighborhood in Cambridge, Massachusetts. The man had locked himself out of his house and was attempting to get back in his home. A neighbor called the police thinking a potential burglary was in progress. The police showed up and the man refused to identify himself and was arrested.

Obama said the following regarding the incident, "I don't know, not having been there and not seeing all the facts, what role race played in that. But I think it's fair to say, number one, any of us would be pretty angry; number two, that the Cambridge police acted stupidly in arresting somebody when there was already proof that they were in their own home, and, number three, what I think we know separate and apart from this incident is that there's a long history in this country of African Americans and Latinos being stopped by law enforcement disproportionately."

The president of the United States stated that the police acted stupidly for arresting a man for not identifying himself who was breaking into a home. The police would not know if the man lives in the home, unless he identified himself. If that was my neighborhood and someone was attempting to get into a house without a key, I would hope someone would call the police. What did Obama do with the biggest bully pulpit in America? Obama created division between the black community and the police. He was basically telling the black community, you do not have to listen or identify yourself when confronted by the police.

Blue Lives Matter

After this incident and in recent years, there has been organized hostility against the police by the Democrat Party and Black Lives Matter (a Democrat organization). They paint the police with one broad brush, because of the actions of a few bad police officers. This hostility creates division, anger and jealousy. I have seen countless videos of police pulling over black men and the men refusing to listen to police instructions. As a result, a struggle ensues, there is violence and sometimes people are killed. I have also seen the same with white individuals refusing to listen to police instructions and the same struggles and violence occurs. However, there are no protests for these encounters, because it does not fit the Democrat scheme. The Democrat Party portrays the police as bad and as a result, minorities are defying the police and it is creating a division… The Democrat Party has the same goal as Satan, which is division, chaos and rebellion.

The Bible also says, *"Therefore whoever resists the authority resists the ordinance of God, and those who resist will bring judgment on themselves. For rulers are not a terror to good works, but to evil. Do you want to be unafraid of the authority? Do what is good, and you will have praise from the same. For he is God's minister to you for good. But if you do evil, be afraid; for he does not bear the sword in vain; for he is God's minister, an avenger to execute wrath on him who practices evil. Therefore you must be subject, not only because of wrath but also for conscience' sake."* (Romans 13:2-5)

The Bible says we should respect authority. We are to not speak evil of anyone, be peaceable, gentle and be humble. If you follow these rules, you will have no problem when dealing with authority, including the police. The encounters with the police that go horribly wrong are argumentative, aggressive, disrespectful and prideful.

Peace is not the Goal of the Democrat Party
There is something very dangerous about this scheme of division, victimization and blame by the Democrat Party. As I stated, it creates jealousy which leads to resentment and anger. If a conservative or Christian is allowed to speak on a college campus, they will be shouted down, there will be violent protests by angry liberals and Democrats. Conservative Supreme Court justices get shouted down during confirmation hearings. Republican President Donald Trump supporters have been called everything from "deplorable" by

Democrat Hillary Clinton to the "dregs of society" by Democrat Joe Biden. Trump supports have been attacked for wearing MAGA hats. The anger and violence is so bad that Trump supporters will not wear shirts with his name or put his bumper stickers on their cars out of fear of being attacked.

The Democrat scheme is creating jealousy, resentment and anger. These mixes of emotions also lead people to commit murder. There are coworkers who believe they were treated unfairly, they become jealous and resentful, get angry and go into their job and murder coworkers. Jealous husbands get angry and murder their spouses. There are stories every day in the news of people committing murder over a pair of sneakers, a necklace, car and money. Those committing these acts are jealous and angry over what others have. James Allen said, "The strife of the world in all its forms, whether it be war, social or political quarrelling, sectarian hatred, private disputes or commercial competition, has its origin in one common cause, namely, individual selfishness."

The First Murder can be Traced to Jealousy and Anger.
The Bible says that first murder that ever occurred was when Cain killed Abel. It was due to jealousy and anger.

The Bible says, *"Now Adam knew Eve his wife, and she conceived and bore Cain, and said, 'I have acquired a man from the Lord.' Then she bore again, this time his brother Abel. Now Abel was a keeper of sheep, but Cain was a tiller of the ground. And in the process of time it came to pass that Cain brought an offering of the fruit of the ground to the Lord. Abel also brought of the firstborn of his flock and of their fat. And the Lord respected Abel and his offering, but He did not respect Cain and his offering. And Cain was very angry, and his countenance fell. So the Lord said to Cain, 'Why are you angry? And why has your countenance fallen? If you do well, will you not be accepted? And if you do not do well, sin lies at the door. And its desire is for you, but you should rule over it.' Now Cain talked with Abel his brother; and it came to pass, when they were in the field, that Cain rose up against Abel his brother and killed him."* (Genesis 4:1-8)

The Bible says that Cain and Abel both gave an offering to God. However, God respected the offering from Abel, because he gave the first born of the flock. Caine's offering was given in time and so it was not respected by God. Cain became jealous of Abel even though it was his own actions that caused God not to respect him. Cain was in disobedience to God. He was not giving to God as he was required. As a result, Cain killed his brother out of jealous anger.

Take notice of what God said to Cain before the murder? God asked Cain why he was upset. God tells Cain that if he does well that he will be accepted. But if he does not, sin lies at the door. God tells Cain to rule over sin. However, Cain does not and covets the respect God gives to Able. He is jealous and angry, and it leads to murder.

The results of the Democrat Party platform are very similar to the actions of Cain. Democrats believe they do not have to follow God's Word and that they can do as they please. When their lives are not as prosperous as those who live for God, they covet what others have, get jealous and strike out in anger.

The Democrat Party's message is the exact opposite of the word of God. They do not preach personal responsibility and to do well. They preach irresponsibility, victimization and blame. The truth is that the power to do well is within everyone's hands. There is opportunity for everyone in America. If you are poor, there are grants (free money) for school as well as loans for school. There are jobs if you are willing to work. There are choices you can make on how you want to live. There is the choice to live according to the word of God or not. The power to do well is within every person's hands.

Crime Results from the Democrat Party Platform not Race
Statistics show that black men commit nearly half of all murders in America, which is astonishing when you consider they account for a small percent of the population. The majority of the murders also occur in metropolitan areas such as St. Louis, Baltimore, Detroit, Chicago, Washington, DC. These metropolitan areas are run and have been run by the Democrat Party for decades. Statistics show that Democrats receive over 90% of the black vote. Pine Hills, Florida where minorities were the majority. Was called "Crime Hills", because of the drugs, crime, violence and murder. In the local Congressional election there, Republicans do not even run, because they have no chance. Democrats run unopposed. This means that blacks affiliate with the Democrat Party and their message (scheme).

As I stated, that message (scheme) is division, jealousy and anger…
The high murder rates in metropolitan areas that are committed by
minorities have nothing to do with race and everything to do with
Democrat Party affiliation.

The Biblical Answer to Leveling the Playing Field and Reducing the Wealth Gap

The Biblical answer to fraudulent proposal of leveling the playing
field and resolving the wealth gap is to just live according to your
means. It does not matter if you make $24,000 a year or $240,000 a
year, if you do not live within your means you are headed for
financial disaster. The Bible warns us to not to lay up our treasures
here on earth.

The Bible says, *"Do not lay up for yourselves treasures on earth, where
moth and rust destroy and where thieves break in and steal; but lay up for
yourselves treasures in heaven, where neither moth nor rust destroys and where
thieves do not break in and steal. For where your treasure is, there your heart will
be also."* (Matthew 6:19-21)

There are people who earn $24,000 a year that are living according
to their means and live content lives. There are also people who earn
$240,000 a year and do not live according to their means and live a
life of stress and torment. I have lived on both ends of this spectrum
and I can tell you that I am much happier living within my means
earning less money, than stressing to pay for a life of excess.

Many years ago, before I turned my life over to the Lord, I
worked in financial services and made a lot of money. Some of my
jobs included a Financial Advisor at Morgan Stanley, a supervisor at
the Bank of New York and managing risk at E*Trade. I drove an
expensive sports car, owned an expensive house and filled it with
expensive furniture. I was laying up for myself treasures here on
earth. I thought my value was in my possessions. When I look back,
it was the worst time of my life… If I had been knowledgeable about
the word of God, I would have known this and saved myself much
heartache and pain. Solomon, the richest man who ever lived said,
"Vanity of vanities," says the Preacher; *"Vanity of vanities, all is vanity." What
profit has a man from all his labor In which he toils under the sun?"*
(Ecclesiastes 1:2-3)

It was a foolish existence that I was living. Toiling away every day, because I cared about what others would think of me, based on what I possessed. I was trying to impress others and I was living with no peace. It was a trap by Satan. I was in bondage…

The Bible says, *"The fear of man brings a snare, But whoever trusts in the Lord shall be safe."* (Proverbs 29:25)

This scripture means worrying about what others think about you is a trap and that you should just trust in the Lord. When I turned my life over to God, He did some major pruning that I was unwilling to do. It was then that my life changed. Now, I own a modest car and house and I do not care what others think of my possession. I earn one-third of the income that I once earned, but I am happy! I no longer lay up treasure on earth. I lay up treasure in heaven and I feel richer than when I had more possessions.

The Bible says, *"There is one who makes himself rich, yet has nothing; And one who makes himself poor, yet has great riches."* (Proverbs 13:7)

The Bible says Do Not Covet

How do you live according to your means? The Bible gives the answer. It is being content with what you have. It is in direct contrast to the Democrat Party's message of resolving the wealth gap and leveling the playing field monetarily. When the Democrat Party pushes their scheme, it does something else. It causes covetousness. The definition of covet is to desire what belongs to another. Cain killed Abel out of jealousy, because he coveted (desired) the relationship that Abel had with God. The scheme of victimization and blame creates jealousy of what others have, which leads to coveting. The tenth commandment says, "you shall not covet". What is coveting? Coveting is a strong desire for what belongs to someone else. Deuteronomy 5:21 goes in greater detail. It says, *"You shall not covet your neighbor's wife; and you shall not desire your neighbor's house, his field, his male servant, his female servant, his ox, his donkey, or anything that is your neighbor's."*
This means that you shall not covet (desire) what belongs to your neighbor. It is okay to want a nice car, but you should be happy that

your neighbor has a nice car and not covet (desire) his car. The Bible says a man finds a good thing when he finds a wife. It is good to want a wife, but you should not covet (desire) your neighbor's wife.

Who is Your Neighbor?
The Bible says that you shall not covet anything that is your neighbors. That raises the question, who is your neighbor? Let me define neighbor for you. When Jesus said to love your neighbor as yourself the disciples asked who is your neighbor? Jesus then gave the parable of the Good Samaritan. To avoid giving a detailed theological explanation, I will tell you that a neighbor is anyone that you encounter. As a result, you should not desire anything that belongs to someone that you are in contact with.

Lastly, Jesus tells us to beware of covetousness and that life does not consist of possession.

The Bible says, *"And He said to them, "Take heed and beware of covetousness, for one's life does not consist in the abundance of the things he possesses."* (Luke 12:1)

The Bible not only tells you not to covet, but to be content (satisfied), with what you have. The opposite of coveting is being content.

The Bible says, *"Let your conduct be without covetousness; be content with such things as you have. For He Himself has said, "I will never leave you nor forsake you."* (Hebrews 13:5)

An example of how coveting led to murder in the Bible. King Ahab coveted (desired) a vineyard owned by a man named Naboth. King Ahab already had a palace. However, he desired this man's vineyard. King Ahab asked Naboth to sell him the vineyard but Naboth refused. It eventually led to the murder of Naboth in a plot by Jezebel, King Ahab's wife to obtain the vineyard. However, Jezebel's life eventually came to a very gruesome ending. To this day, no one names their child Jezebel.
Resolving the wealth gap by the Democrat Party is a message of coveting what other people have. It is a message of not to be content

with what you have, but desire what belongs to your neighbor. It creates jealousy and anger all of which is not Godly.

The Bible says, *"Now godliness with contentment is great gain. For we brought nothing into this world, and it is certain we can carry nothing out. And having food and clothing, with these we shall be content. But those who desire to be rich fall into temptation and a snare, and into many foolish and harmful lusts which drown men in destruction and perdition. For the love of money is a root of all kinds of evil, for which some have strayed from the faith in their greediness, and pierced themselves through with many sorrows."* (1 Timothy 6:6-11)

Forgiveness

There will be times in life when you will be wronged. It happens to everyone. There is a choice we must make when we are wronged. First let me say, if it is criminal wrong, you should seek justice. However, because someone earns more than you or has a bigger house that is not criminal. In all circumstances, the answer is not to get jealous, angry or get even. The Biblical answer when you have been wronged or mistreated is to forgive.

George Hebert said, "He that cannot forgive others, breaks the bridge over which he himself must pass if he would ever reach heaven; for everyone has need to be forgiven." I once read something Rick Warren wrote that I will never forget. He said, "you will never be asked to forgive someone else more than God has forgiven you." It is true. We all are sinners and in the span of our lifetimes, we will commit more sins that God will have to forgive us for than we will have to forgive any one single person for sinning against us. Someone may cut you off in traffic, but God is going to have to forgive you for much more than that....

The quote by Rick Warren is a paraphrase of the Unforgiving Servant, a parable by Jesus. It is recorded in Matthew 18:21-35. I challenge you to read it. When I explain it to people, I bring it to modern day terms. I explain it like this. If you borrowed one million dollars from a rich man, but when he came to collect it, you could not pay him. You had spent the money foolishly. The rich man out of compassion forgave your debt anyway. You were forgiven of all that you owed. You walked away free of that debt. However, on your way home, you came across someone that had borrowed just ten dollars from you. When you asked for the ten dollars back, the person could not pay you. You then had him beaten and thrown into a prison. You that just had a million dollars forgiven, but would not forgive someone owing you $10. What kind of person are you? Well, that is us if we do not forgive others. God will forgive you of every sin you have ever committed, you just have to forgive those who have sinned against you.

The Bible says, *"But if you do not forgive men their trespasses, neither will your Father forgive your trespasses."* (Matthew 6:15)

Jesus Forgives on the Cross

Jesus is our example and you will never have to forgive anyone more than when Jesus forgave those that crucified Him. Jesus committed no sin. Yet, He was beaten scourged, tortured and hung on a cross to die. As He hung on the cross dying, He forgave…

The Bible says, *"Then Jesus said, "Father, forgive them, for they do not know what they do."* (Luke 23:34)

As Christians we are called to forgive. Anytime that you think you cannot forgive someone for a wrong done to you, think of Jesus on the cross, offering forgiveness.

Jealousy and Abortion

I want to come back to the topic of abortion in this chapter. The Bible shows that jealousy and coveting lead to resentment and anger which leads to murder. There are over a half a million abortions every year in the United Sates. As a man, I cannot get pregnant or have an abortion, so I decided to research the top reasons that women have abortions. The top reasons are as follows:

1. Financial instability: The inability to support or care for a child. This is jealousy, resenting that others will have more than you and that your child will not have as much as others have.

2. Negative impact on the mother's life: Interfere with the mother's work, social life or schooling. This is jealousy and coveting the activities of others.

3. The mother does not want to be a single parent. This is
    jealousy and resentment of too much of a workload. It is
    coveting the leisure (interfere with the single lifestyle) and
    relationships that others have (difficult to find a husband).

All the reasons given for having abortions can be classified under
jealousy, resentment and coveting what others have. Jealousy,
resentment and coveting lead to anger and anger leads to murder.
What is abortion? It is murder!

IX

THE PROGRESSIVE INCOME TAX SYSTEM

Satan Appears as an Angel of Light- Higher tax rates on the wealthy are needed to right the wrongs done to the poor and oppressed in society. The rich need to pay their fair share.

Satan's Goal: Penalize success and reward laziness which leads to destruction.

What does the Bible say? The *"Parable of the Talents"* in Matthew 25:14–30

Once the Democrat Party proposes to create a level playing field, (which is not possible to achieve), they must fund it. The only way to do this is to implement a progressive tax system, which taxes people at a higher rate for making greater amounts of money. The more successful a person is, the more they are required to pay. It is a system that rewards laziness and punishes success.

Democrat President Barack Obama said, "I would look at raising the capital-gains tax for purposes of fairness."

Democrat Hillary Clinton said, "The rich are not paying their fair share in any nation that is facing the kind of employment issues (the United States is), whether it's individual, corporate, whatever the taxation forms are."

Democrat Bernie Sanders said, "It is appropriate to ask the wealthy and large corporations to start paying their fair share of taxes."

It seems compassionate, to make the wealthy pay more to help the poor. However, there is not enough money to transfer from the ultra-wealthy to solve the problem of poverty. If you look at this logically, it penalizes those that work hard. It penalizes success.

If you had a child that was given 5 chores to do in a week (all chores were equal work) and you gave your child $5 for the first chore, $4 for the second, $3 for the third, $2 for the fourth and $1 for the last chore. What would be the incentive to do complete all 5 chores? The child just might stop at the third chore? At some point, the child will determine it is not worth working so hard to get everything done… Take this another step, say that the child did all 5 chores and was paid the $15. If that child had a sibling and the sibling received $10 as an allowance for doing nothing, what would be the incentive for the first child to do any chores at all? It would be better just to take the $10 for doing nothing.

Let me make this even more simple to understand. If you have two children, wouldn't you reward a child that worked hard doing chores and punish a child that was lazy, goofing off and doing no chores? It would be foolish and counterproductive if you cared about your children to punish the hard-working child and reward the lazy child…

Take this example to sports. In professional sports, players are given incentives to achieve. If a player hits so many home runs or makes an all-star team they receive incentive bonuses. What if that system was reversed and players were taxed (penalized) for hitting more home runs or making an all-star team and money was given to the players that underperformed, did not practice or show up for the games. Players would fail on purpose. The game itself would be compromised and discredited to the point of extinction….

This is exactly what a progressive tax system does. It penalizes for hard work, for doing more and for succeeding. Thomas Sowell said, "One of the sad signs of our times is that we have demonized those who produce, subsidized those who refuse to produce, and canonized those who complain." Republicans have proposed a flat tax for many years as a compromise, however, Democrats portray it as unfair. Let me tell you what is unfair. It is taxing someone more for achieving and succeeding.

Nothing Good is Ever Results from Laziness

In my fifty plus years on earth, I have not seen anything good that ever resulted from laziness. However, I have seen plenty of bad things that have resulted from it. I have seen people fail in school. I have seen people get fired from their jobs for being late or not getting their work done. I have seen people not reach their potential in life. I have seen poor health conditions in people. I have seen people in poverty, including homelessness. Benjamin Franklin said, "laziness travels so slowly that poverty soon overtakes it." The book of Proverbs has a lot to say about laziness….

"The soul of a lazy man desires, and has nothing; But the soul of the diligent shall be made rich." (Proverbs 13:4)

"He who has a slack hand becomes poor, But the hand of the diligent makes rich." (Proverbs 10:4)

"In all labor there is profit, But idle chatter leads only to poverty." (Proverbs 14:23)

"The lazy man will not plow because of winter; He will beg during harvest and have nothing." (Proverbs 20:4)

"Laziness casts one into a deep sleep, And an idle person will suffer hunger." (Proverbs 19:15)

"Do not love sleep, lest you come to poverty; Open your eyes, and you will be satisfied with bread." (Proverbs 20:13)

The Bible says that laziness will lead to hunger and poverty. The question then becomes, why would the Democrat Party want to reward laziness? Again, the Democrat Party wants you to become dependent on them and in poverty you will. Secondly, the Democrat Party (like Satan) does not want you bearing good fruit and doing good works. They want you wasting your life and gifts that God has given you.

The Bible says, *"that you may walk worthy of the Lord, fully pleasing*

Him, being fruitful in every good work and increasing in the knowledge of God."
(Colossians 1:10)

This means that you are to live a life worthy of the God, pleasing Him and being fruitful in every good work.

The Parable of the Talents
The Biblical argument against the progressive income tax is found in the Parable of the Talents by Jesus. I am going to include the entire parable below and then comment on it. Talent in this scripture is a unit of value. However, the origin of the use of the word "talent" to mean "gift or skill" comes from this scripture.

The Bible says, *"For the kingdom of heaven is like a man traveling to a far country, who called his own servants and delivered his goods to them. And to one he gave five talents, to another two, and to another one, to each according to his own ability; and immediately he went on a journey. Then he who had received the five talents went and traded with them, and made another five talents. And likewise he who had received two gained two more also. But he who had received one went and dug in the ground, and hid his lord's money. After a long time the lord of those servants came and settled accounts with them.*
"So he who had received five talents came and brought five other talents, saying, 'Lord, you delivered to me five talents; look, I have gained five more talents besides them.' His lord said to him, 'Well done, good and faithful servant; you were faithful over a few things, I will make you ruler over many things. Enter into the joy of your lord.' He also who had received two talents came and said, 'Lord, you delivered to me two talents; look, I have gained two more talents besides them.' His lord said to him, 'Well done, good and faithful servant; you have been faithful over a few things, I will make you ruler over many things. Enter into the joy of your lord.' "Then he who had received the one talent came and said, 'Lord, I knew you to be a hard man, reaping where you have not sown, and gathering where you have not scattered seed. And I was afraid, and went and hid your talent in the ground. Look, there you have what is yours.' "But his lord answered and said to him, 'You wicked and lazy servant, you knew that I reap where I have not sown, and gather where I have not scattered seed. So you ought to have deposited my money with the bankers, and at my coming I would have received back my own with interest. Therefore take the talent from him, and give it to him who has ten talents. For to everyone who has, more will be given, and he will have abundance; but from him who does not have, even what he has will be

taken away. And cast the unprofitable servant into the outer darkness. There will be weeping and gnashing of teeth." (Matthew 25:14-30)

The parable tells us that God gives you gifts to accomplish His work on earth. It is then up to you to use those gifts. God holds you accountable on how you use your gifts. You have the choice to use your gifts or do nothing with them. God rewards those that accomplish and who do well. God is so serious about accomplishing and not being lazy that He takes from those who squander their gifts and gives it to those who produce. Ultimately, the reward is great for those that use the gifts they are given. For those that do not use their gifts, there is great punishment. The progressive tax plan is a cornerstone of the Democrat Party and contradictory to how God rewards those that produce and accomplish.

The Death Tax
The Death Tax is another example of a platform by the Democrat that is not Biblical. The death tax imposes a tax on estates when people die when they are over a certain value. This means that if you produce and achieve, during your life, your family will be punished. If you do not produce and achieve over the course of your lifetime, your family is safe. The Democrat Party believes that if you have done well in life you must give part of that fortune to the government. This tax is supported by the Democrat Party and it takes from people who have succeeded and accomplished greatly in life. It is a tax to punish a lifetime of success.

Punishing Success Destroys
How would God accomplish His work on earth if He punished hard workers and rewarded those that are lazy? If this is how God ran the church, the church would have failed a long time ago. Again, this is what the Democrat Party wants for America. They want America, freedom and success to fail. It is the reason the punish success and reward failure. The Parable of the Talents shows once again, the Democrat Party platform is not Biblical.

X

WEALTH REDISTRIBUTION

Satan Appears as an Angel of Light: We, the government, must redistribute money from the successful and wealthy to the poor and disadvantaged to right the wrongs of society. It is the Parable of the Good Samaritan and the Bible says, *"I am my brother's keeper."*

Satan's Goal: Reward laziness and unproductivity, which leads to dependence.

What does the Bible say? *"You shall not steal."* (Exodus 20:15)

Once the Democrat Party has implemented a progressive tax scheme of taking money from producers in society, it then redistributes the money in various schemes to obtain and also retain power. The money is given to special interest groups that support their agenda such as Planned Parenthood, labor unions, public radio, the arts… It is also used to purchase votes from individuals in the form of government handouts.

Let me be clear, there are good reasons to help certain individuals. There are individuals with developmental disabilities, there are children that need assistance, people who have medical issues, elderly that need care and there are people who have lost their jobs. I have worked with individuals with developmental disabilities and planted a church in a poverty-stricken city. I have seen people in despair.

One afternoon, while doing ministry in Pine Hills, I stopped in a Hardees in the center of the city. A couple, both in their mid-thirties, pushing a baby in a stroller came in to the restaurant. The man was in an old t-shirt, shorts and poorly groomed. The woman looked to be in her thirties. She had a scar from a tracheotomy done at some point in her life and she was blind in one eye. This couple needed help... There was a social worker in the restaurant counseling them. These are the people that need the help from the government and do not truly get it, because too many that are getting government handouts that are mentally and physically capable of working.

Today, government handouts have expanded far beyond helping those in need. Today you can receive monthly handouts for welfare, food, housing, phones, electricity and more. Thomas Sowell said, "The old adage about giving a man a fish versus teaching him to fish has been updated by a reader: Give a man a fish and he will ask for tartar sauce and French fries!" Moreover, some politician who wants his vote will declare all these things to be among his "basic rights."

In 2018, the liberal Democrat mayor of Stockton, California has implemented a policy for paying criminals not to commit crimes. Low-income cash monthly payments are paid to men that are likely to commit violent crimes. After pastoring a church in a low-income minority neighborhood, I can tell you that most of the crime is committed by young men, gangs or is drug related. If you just give free money to these people, with no responsibility attached, you would just be aiding them in committing more and larger crimes.

A large centralized federal government also spends money on a lot of wasteful projects. For more than 20 years, Northwestern University researchers received National Institutes of Health money to watch hamster fights. The project reportedly received more than $3 million over the course of the project. There are thousands of examples like this. There is something called the annual Congressional Pig Book that lists government wasteful projects and studies. A quick search of the Internet and you can read the billions of dollars in wasteful federal government spending.

The Federal government also sends hundreds of millions of dollars a year to other countries. Some of these countries are declared enemies of America. If this does not explicitly demonstrate that the Democrat Party wants America to fail nothing else will. How can anyone justify sending money to enemies that want to destroy you. It is a flawed pattern of thinking. Democrat Present Barrack Obama sent $1.7 billion dollars in cash to Iran, a country who main purpose is to destroy Israel and America. Would not it be wiser to strengthen your own country and take care of your own citizens first?

Democrats Twist the Word of God

The Democrat party again twists the word of God when it comes to wealth redistribution. They say for government to take from the wealthy and give to the poor is in accordance with the Bible and that Jesus was a liberal Democrat. Nothing could be further from the truth! In previous chapters, I quoted the scriptures about the importance of caring for your family, laziness and if you do not work that you should not eat. Nowhere in the Bible are any scriptures related to government forcibly taking wealth from anyone and redistributing it to others in need.

My Brother's Keeper

In reference to helping others, Democrat President Barrack Obama said, "But part of that belief comes from my faith in the idea that I am my brother's keeper and I am my sister's keeper; that as a country, we rise and fall together. I'm not an island."

Let us take a look at the scripture. What does the Bible really say about being my "brother's keeper"? After Cain murdered Abel out of jealousy God asked Cain where his brother was...

The Bible says, *"Then the Lord said to Cain, "Where is Abel your brother?" He said, "I do not know. Am I my brother's keeper?" And He said, "What have you done? The voice of your brother's blood cries out to Me from the ground."* (Genesis 4:8-10)

Cain had just murdered his brother Abel out of jealous anger and God asked Cain where his brother was. Cain responded, *"am I my brother's keeper?"* How do you interpret this scripture to mean that we are to care for others in society? Cain gave this reply to God as an excuse and to hide his crime of murder. The response was a lie, because Cain knew where his brother was, he murdered him. What did Obama do? He twisted the word of God. He used that same phrase to deflect from the truth and lie like Cain. Those who do not know the Bible believed him. Again, if you do not know the word of God, you will be fooled into believing things and taking actions contrary to God's will.

The Good Samaritan

The other scripture Democrats use to defend wealth redistribution is the parable of the Good Samaritan. Let's look at that scripture. A Samaritan on his travels, found a man lying on the side of the road that was attacked by robbers. The man was injured, and everything was taken from him. The Samaritan saw the man and helped him.

The Bible says, *"So he went to him and bandaged his wounds, pouring on oil and wine; and he set him on his own animal, brought him to an inn, and took care of him. On the next day, when he departed, he took out two denarii, gave them to the innkeeper, and said to him, 'Take care of him; and whatever more you spend, when I come again, I will repay you.' So which of these three do you think was neighbor to him who fell among the thieves?" And he said, "He who showed mercy on him." Then Jesus said to him, "Go and do likewise."* (Luke 10:34-37)

The Parable of the Good Samaritan tells us to show mercy and compassion on those we meet that are suffering, hurt or have encountered misfortune. The Samaritan helped a man that was injured in very poor condition. The injuries were not of the man's own accord, but the result of being robbed and beaten. Notice that the Samaritan only helped the injured man temporarily, until he became healthy. If you were beaten, robbed and injured on the side of the road, I am certain you would want someone passing by to help you. That is what Jesus wants of us. Give a helping hand to those in need that we encounter and make them well. However, the Democrat Party twists the scripture to mean endless government handouts for all, including healthy people who can work.

The Eighth Commandment

Wealth redistribution is the government legislating taking money, or property from one person and giving it to another. Democrats are a party that believes in wealth redistribution. To put this in perspective if a private citizen did this, it would be called stealing.

Teddy Roosevelt said, "The eighth commandment reads, "Thou shalt not steal." It does not read, "Thou shalt not steal from the rich man." It does not read, "Thou shalt not steal from the poor man." It reads simply and plainly, "Thou shalt not steal."

Thomas Sowell said, "I have never understood why it is "greed" to want to keep the money you have earned but not greed to want to take somebody else's money."

Walter Williams said, "No matter how worthy the cause, it is robbery, theft, and injustice to confiscate the property of one person and give it to another to whom it does not belong.".

Williams also said…., "For the Christians among us, socialism and the welfare state must be seen as sinful. When God gave Moses the commandment, Thou shalt not steal, I'm sure He didn't mean thou shalt not steal unless there's a majority vote. And I'm sure that if you asked God if it's OK just being a recipient of stolen property, He would deem that a sin as well."

The eighth commandment in the Bible says, *You shall not steal.*

Democrats Want to Steal the Blessings from Working and Giving

The Blessings of Work

The Bible warns against not working and the Bible also tells of the blessings associated with working. The Bible tells us that God worked. God created the heavens and earth in six days and on the seventh day He rested. Jesus also worked while He was here on earth doing the Will of His Father. If you want to know what a day in the life of Jesus was like, read Matthew 14. The chapter describes an entire day in the life of Jesus. Jesus worked from morning until late in the night. Jesus did not receive any government handouts.

There are blessings that come from working. Work creates products, time is used positively, learning occurs, relationships develop, prosperity is created to care for family and others. Every job is honorable. The Democrat Party is so anti-biblical, not only will they keep you trapped on government handouts that they even oppose work requirements for those on government handouts. Although, written more than 2,000 years ago, anyone working today, should be able to testify to that truth that working brings blessings.

Samuel Smiles said, "It has been truly said, that to desire to possess, without being burdened with the trouble of acquiring, is as much a sign of weakness, as to recognize that everything worth having is only to be got by paying its price, is the prime secret of practical strength. Even leisure cannot be enjoyed unless it is won by effort. If it have not been earned by work, the price has not been paid for it."

The Bible says, *"When you eat the labor of your hands, You shall be happy, and it shall be well with you."* (Psalm 128:2)

The Bible says, *"Nothing is better for a man than that he should eat and drink, and that his soul should enjoy good in his labor. This also, I saw, was from the hand of God."* (Ecclesiastes 2:24)

The Blessings I Received from Working

I have had many jobs in my life and I received countless blessing from those jobs. I earned wages, learned life lessons, developed character and discipline, and made relationships from each job. Wages protected me from homelessness and always allowed me to have food to eat. Working allowed me to gain wisdom about investing and the financial markets. I learned practical things that helped me in life. Working developed good habits of polite interaction and respecting authority and doing things efficiently. It developed discipline of being on time and getting work finished timely. Working allowed me to make great friends. One of those includes, a coworker that invited me to church that led to me dedicating my life to the Lord. That is a priceless blessing.

It takes a lifetime of experiences and learning to gain wisdom. Most people associate work with money. I can tell you one of the greatest blessings I ever received was at a job where I received very little pay. As I stated, I worked in a Day Program with individuals with developmental disabilities and that these individuals teach you to appreciate the blessing that you have and about unconditional love. They also taught me another valuable lesson It is that everyone needs a place to go every day. Everyone also needs to have responsibilities, be held accountable and have relationships.

Calvin Coolidge said, "All growth depends upon activity. There is no development physically or intellectually without effort, and effort means work."

The Bible says, *"Therefore, leaving the discussion of the elementary principles of Christ, let us go on to perfection, not laying again the foundation of repentance from dead works and of faith toward God."* (Hebrews 6:1)

As part of my job duties at the program, I was sent to a home of a young man who was 29 years old with Down's Syndrome. He had become a recluse in his home. I was told that he was anti-social, that he never left his room and refused to go out in public. When I arrived at his house, his mother said that he stopped all social activities and even stopped speaking. She told me that in high school he was popular, he was able to speak and also participated in social activities. Now, he stayed up all night disrupting the family, slept all day and rarely left his bedroom. She did not understand why? When I waked into his bedroom, I immediately knew why...

His mother, out of what she believed was compassion and probably guilt, gave the young man everything that he wanted. She created a Day Program in his own bedroom. He had a large radio system with speakers, musical equipment, a large television, movies, books and his own refrigerator. She made his room so comfortable, with everything he needed that he never wanted to leave it.

As a result, he spent seven years cooped up in his bedroom never wanting to leave. He was subject to no discipline, had no responsibilities, no daily requirements, he had no friends or relationships. He had no communication with anyone except his mother and his young nephews when they visited. As a result, He lost his writing skills, his speaking skills and social skills.

I was once asked to write a letter about the Day program facility where I worked and all the benefits that it provided to the participants that attended the program. I said, "that will be easy!" In the letter, I described the fellowship that all the participants shared with each other. How they had friendships and made best friends and interacted with one another. The facility also offered the opportunity for earning money, learning, maintaining skills.... It also offered activities the individuals would not have otherwise participate in. Activities such as bowling outings, shopping at thrift stores, arcades, parks, video games… The facility gave the participants a chance at life. When they walked in to the facility each morning, they gave you hugs and high fives! Compare that to the average person that walks onto their job every morning! The facility was a blessing and provided blessings!

Although, the young man I went to see had Down's Syndrome, he still needed the discipline of a daily routine. He needed a place to go, he needed to be wanted in some capacity and held accountable for his actions. He also needed relationships and fellowship. If this young man with Down's Syndrome needed these things, how much more does an able-bodied individual with no disabilities need them?

However, that is not in the platform (scheme) of the Democrat Party. Their agenda with regards to those who are able bodied and have no physical or mental barriers to work is to provide them endless government handouts. As a result, it denies the many blessings that come with working.

The Blessings of Giving

The Bible directly addresses the issue of individuals and not government willingly making a personal decision of giving money to help others in need. God judges us on our giving and we receive blessings for what we do. Once again, if it was possible for every person to have the same and all your needs were cared for, there is one problem… How are people to give? Your giving would be limited by what the government gives you and your blessings would also be limited. The Bible calls on you to work and to help others.

The Bible says, *"Let him who stole steal no longer, but rather let him labor, working with his hands what is good, that he may have something to give him who has need."* (Ephesians 4:28)

We are to work and earn an honest living to provide for our families and to help others... We are to give to others in need and when we do, we receive blessings for it.

The Bible says, *"But this I say: He who sows sparingly will also reap sparingly, and he who sows bountifully will also reap bountifully. So let each one give as he purposes in his heart, not grudgingly or of necessity; for God loves a cheerful giver."* (2 Corinthians 9:6-7)

The Bible says, *"I have shown you in every way, by laboring like this, that you must support the weak. And remember the words of the Lord Jesus, that He said, It is more blessed to give than to receive."* (Acts 20:35)

The Bible says that you will reap according to what you give. It also says it is more blessed to give than to receive. The Democrat Party with a platform contrary to God, wants to steal (take away) the blessings of working and giving that God has for you. We are to give what our heart decides, because God tests us and will judge us by the choices we make.

Zac Poonen said, "God tests us in the matter of receiving and giving to see whether we desire to live by the principles of the world or of His kingdom."

The Bible says, *"I, the Lord, search the heart, I test the mind, Even to give every man according to his ways, According to the fruit of his doings."* (Jeremiah 17:10)

There will be even greater blessings that you will receive than the ones here on earth, because these are only temporary. Heaven promises eternal blessings unlike anything you can imagine.

The Bible says, *"But as it is written: Eye has not seen, nor ear heard, Nor have entered into the heart of man The things which God has prepared for those who love Him."* (1 Corinthians 2:9)

How you spend eternity should be of great concern to you. The Bible says that we are saved by faith but judged by our works. Your faith determines where you will spend eternity. If you accept Jesus as our Lord and Savior, you will spend eternity in heaven. The next question is how do you spend that eternity in Heaven? The Bible says there are rewards given in heaven for the work you do on earth. The Bible describes five crowns that a believer can earn. These crowns are the Imperishable Crown, the Crown of Rejoicing, the Crown of Righteousness, the Crown of Glory, and the Crown of Life. As a result, what you do with your time here on earth matters. You will stand before Christ when your life as done as a believer and your works on earth will be judged.

The Bible says, *"For we must all appear before the judgment seat of Christ, that each one may receive the things done in the body, according to what he has done, whether good or bad."* (2 Corinthians 5:10)

XI

THE IDOLATRY OF GOVERNMENT

Satan Appears as an Angel of Light: Place your cares and trust in us, the government. We, the government, will provide you with everything that you need in life including food, shelter and clothing. We will eliminate mistreatment and injustice.

Satan's Goal: Replace God in your life with government.

What does the Bible say?

"To you it was shown, that you might know that the Lord Himself is God; there is none other besides Him." (Deuteronomy 4:35)

"There Is No Other God "Thus says the Lord, the King of Israel, And his Redeemer, the Lord of hosts: 'I am the First and I am the Last; Besides Me there is no God." (Isaiah 44:6)

"For even if there are so-called gods, whether in heaven or on earth (as there are many gods and many lords), yet for us there is one God, the Father, of whom are all things, and we for Him; and one Lord Jesus Christ, through whom are all things, and through whom we live." (1 Corinthians 8:5-6)

Everything the Democrat Party does centers around one specific goal, the idolatry of government. Idolatry is the worship of idols. It is the excessive devotion or reverence for some person or thing as a god. An idol is anything that replaces the one, true God in your life. The idolatry of government. It is where everything begins and ends with the Democrat Party. If they become a god (a false one) to you and you worship them, you will not need anything else. People make

119

false gods (idols) out of all kinds of things. People worship sports stars, reality stars, movie stars, money, work, possessions, cars, houses and even natural things such as the earth. You can add the Democrat Party to that list. The only difference is the intent of the Democrat Party to be a god in your life. The idolatry of government is the entire scheme of the Democrat Party.

As with every important issue impacting the lives of people and society, the Democrat Party, like Satan, is a master of deception. However, in time, the lies and schemes of the Democrat Party are revealed, because their schemes never work. When their schemes fail and get exposed, they just change terms and tactics. Example: Instead of referring to the term government handout (which had negative connotations with time), the Democrat Party came up with a new term: Welfare. Welfare means the health, happiness, and fortunes of a person. This term was used to deceive to associate money given out from government provided health, happiness and fortunes. However, over time that term became associated with people getting endless government checks without having to seek employment. As a result, the Democrat Party changed the terminology again. Welfare then became "Benefits". The definition of benefits is something that produces good or helpful results or that promotes well-being.

Endless benefits without responsibilities does not promote well-being and is not a benefit, it destroys. When the term benefits was exposed as a lie, the terminology was changed once again to "Entitlements". The definition of entitlement is having a right to something. An entitlement constitutes a binding obligation on the part of the federal government. Eligible recipients of entitlement programs have legal recourse if the obligation is not fulfilled. They have a right to money from government.

Today, people that do not work or earn below a certain yearly income now are entitled to money from the government. You need to understand that there are some programs by government that disperse money to individuals such as Social Security that people are entitles to. Social Security pays individuals back at a certain age when they retire, after they paid into it for many years while they worked. As a result, Social Security recipients are entitled to that money. However, with time, entitlements have been perverted to cover much more. Now included under the heading of entitlements is welfare, food stamps, housing subsidies and more…. Any payment you get from the federal government is deemed an entitlement by the Democrat Party, as if a person has a right to it.

I quoted the scripture previously, if a person does not work, neither should he eat. I am going to cite the entire scripture. It is important, because the God says that not only do we have an obligation to work and not be lazy, but we are to be an example to others and we should not even associate with those who refuse to work.

The Bible says, *"But we command you, brethren, in the name of our Lord Jesus Christ, that you withdraw from every brother who walks disorderly and not according to the tradition which he received from us. For you yourselves know how you ought to follow us, for we were not disorderly among you; nor did we eat anyone's bread free of charge, but worked with labor and toil night and day, that we might not be a burden to any of you, not because we do not have authority, but to make ourselves an example of how you should follow us. For even when we were with you, we commanded you this: If anyone will not work, neither shall he eat. For we hear that there are some who walk among you in a disorderly manner, not working at all, but are busybodies. Now those who are such we command and exhort through our Lord Jesus Christ that they work in quietness and eat their own bread. But as for you, brethren, do not grow weary in doing good. And if anyone does not obey our word in this epistle, note that person and do not keep company with him, that he may be ashamed."* (2 Thessalonians 3:6-14)

The Answer to Poverty is not the Government

In the chapter regarding how progressive taxation is not Godly, I cited the Parable of the Talents. God gives us all talents and we are to use those talents and God will bless (reward) us. If you want to leave poverty the answer is to use your talents and not hide and bury them. It is to get an education, work and manage what God has given you in a wise manner. These are Godly principles. Follow the examples of Ben Carson, Herman Cain, Colin Powell, Clarence Thomas and Condoleezza Rice. However, what does the Democrat Party say about these individuals? As previously noted, they mock, ridicule and marginalize them. When a real solution is provided to solve a problem in society such as poverty, the Democrat Party mocks it, lies about it and twists the truth, because they do not desire a solution that rewards you.

Hillary Clinton said, "I call it (Donald Trump's plan) trumped-up trickle-down, because that's exactly what it would be. That is not how we grow the economy."

Barack Obama said, "Now, anybody who thinks that we can move this economy forward with just a few folks at the top doing well, hoping that it's going to trickle down to working people who are running faster and faster just to keep up, you'll never see it."

Democrat Hubert Humphrey said, "My philosophy has always been that benefits should percolate up rather than trickle down."

Trickle Down Economics
Trickle-down economics is the theory that money and benefits in the form of tax cuts trickle down to others in lower economic classes. In this theory, investors, savers, and business are the drivers of growth in an economy. If the successful, wealthy and those who have created businesses are not the drivers of growth, then who is? It certainly is not those sitting around collecting government handouts. They have no resources or have managed their resources so poorly they live in poverty. Only someone desiring disaster would want those in poverty driving an economy.

The Bible is our Example that Trickle-Down Economics Works
The story of Joseph in the Old Testament tells us that trickle-down economics works. Joseph in the book of Genesis was sold into slavery by his brothers to Potiphar, an officer of Pharaoh.

The Bible says, *"Now Joseph had been taken down to Egypt. And Potiphar, an officer of Pharaoh, captain of the guard, an Egyptian, bought him from the Ishmaelites who had taken him down there. The Lord was with Joseph, and he was a successful man; and he was in the house of his master the Egyptian. And his master saw that the Lord was with him and that the Lord made all he did to prosper in his hand. So Joseph found favor in his sight, and served him. Then he made him overseer of his house, and all that he had he put under his authority."* (Genesis 39:1-4)

Although, Joseph was a slave, God was with him and wealth from

Potiphar flowed down to Joseph. Joseph became successful, and he prospered. However, the scriptures state that Potiphar's wife lied and accused Joseph of something that he did not do. When you become successful, you will be attacked and lies will be told about you… Joseph was then thrown into prison. While in prison, Joseph interpreted the dreams of two of pharaoh's servants. One servant told pharaoh that Joseph interpreted a specific dream he had. Joseph was brought out from prison, and accurately interpreted Pharaoh's dream. As a result, he was appointed second-in-command over Egypt.

The Bible says, *"So the advice was good in the eyes of Pharaoh and in the eyes of all his servants. Then Pharaoh said to Joseph, 'Inasmuch as God has shown you all this, there is no one as discerning and wise as you. ⁴⁰You shall be over my house, and all my people shall be ruled according to your word; only in regard to the throne will I be greater than you." And Pharaoh said to Joseph, "See, I have set you over all the land of Egypt." Then Pharaoh took his signet ring off his hand and put it on Joseph's hand; and he clothed him in garments of fine linen and put a gold chain around his neck. And he had him ride in the second chariot which he had; and they cried out before him, "Bow the knee!" So he set him over all the land of Egypt. Pharaoh also said to Joseph, "I am Pharaoh, and without your consent no man may lift his hand or foot in all the land of Egypt."* (Genesis 41:37-44)

Joseph helped the Pharaoh, who ruled over Egypt. In Pharaoh's eyes, no one was as qualified or had the experience and wisdom of Joseph. The pharaoh put Joseph in charge of his affairs and made him second in command of Egypt. Joseph rose from slavery to become successful. He then rose from prison to be second in command over the land of Egypt. It was a trickle-down effect from those that he helped and served that had resources.

Here is what you need to understand, selling to wealthy individuals will earn you more income than selling to people in poverty. People in poverty, do not have money. How else are people in the middle or lower economic levels going to climb the ladder to success? Even if you lack an education, through trickle-down economics you can become successful and wealthy if you work hard. Zig Ziglar said, "You can get everything in life you want if you will just help enough other people get what they want."

He is right! The Bible in the story of Joseph proves it and I can prove it in modern day terms. Would you rather sell a $10,000,000 condominium or a $100,000 house? The commission on the house is $3,000, while the commission on the condo would be $300,000, while both require about the same work. America is filled with endless success stories. I do not care what it is, if you sell enough of anything to someone or help enough people get want they want, you will become wealthy. However, you must work for it. If you were to start a business, would you think it would be better to sell to people in poverty or to millionaires? Millionaires! Walter Williams said, "One of the wonderful things about free markets is that the path to greater wealth comes not from looting, plundering and enslaving one's fellow man, as it has throughout most of human history, but by serving and pleasing him."

The Democrats Trickle Down Plan (Taxation) Does not Work.

The Democrat Party has their own trickle-down plan, it is called taxation and wealth redistribution. It requires no work. Their plan takes from the wealthy and working individuals and redistributes without someone having to earn it. I discussed this in the chapter regarding wealth redistribution.

The Democrat Party trickle down plan of taxation, also leaves out some very important facts. If you give people money, they do not value it, because they have not vested time earning it. Also, if you give people a lot of money that are not good at managing money, they are not going to manage this money properly as well… Individuals that have won the lottery have lost everything in time. Professional athletes and celebrities who have earned tens of millions have lost everything and filed bankruptcy. I was a financial advisor, I have seen people inherit money and within a couple years, it was all gone….

Rush Limbaugh said, The Democrat Party needs a permanent underclass of dependent people to continue to vote to prop Democrats up, and they need more and more of those as people escape lower levels of the middle class or poverty to become more self-reliant. Self-reliance is the biggest enemy the Democrat Party has, and they need to keep supplying the country with essentially a number of people every year that will equate to a permanent underclass that will constantly elect them. That's why they're registering illegals to vote with driver's licenses sign-ups, so forth. So they do want to eliminate the capitalist infrastructure of this country. You don't tell people that's what you're doing. You tell 'em you're engaging in social justice for equality and fairness and to right all these previous injustices that began with the founding of the country from slavery forward. You create the idea that what you're literally doing is establishing a utopia, where there will be no judgmentalism and there will be no unhappiness and there will be no unfairness and there will be no inequality, and there won't be any of the things that upset people. That's how you attract the young. It's working on college campus like a dream right now.

The Bible says, *"Yet we urge you, brothers and sisters, to do so more and more, and to make it your ambition to lead a quiet life: You should mind your own business and work with your hands, just as we told you, so that your daily life may win the respect of outsiders and so that you will not be dependent on anybody."* (1 Thessalonians 4:10-12)

God is Perfect and Government is Not

There is also another problem with making an idol out of government. Government institutions are all imperfect and run by people who are imperfect. Politicians have been known to have selfish motivations and to use power to enrich themselves. Politicians have been known to lie, steal and do unethical things. There is a long list of politicians that have been arrested and sentenced to jail for their actions while in office. It is a mistake to forsake a perfect and loving God (whose Word is truth and never changes) and believe and trust in an imperfect government (that can lie, deceive and enrich itself).

What does the Bible say about the Characteristics of God?

"God is not a man, that He should lie." (Numbers 23:19)

"He is the Rock, His work is perfect; For all His ways are justice, A God of truth and without injustice; Righteous and upright is He. (Deuteronomy 32:4)

"The grass withers, the flower fades, But the word of our God stands forever."

(Isaiah 40:8)

"Not a word failed of any good thing which the Lord had spoken to the house of Israel. All came to pass." (Joshua 21:45)

"As for God, His way is perfect; The word of the Lord is proven; He is a shield to all who trust in Him." (Psalm 18:30)

"Among the gods there is none like You, O Lord; Nor are there any works like Your works." (Psalm 86:8)

"They will perish, but You will endure; Yes, they will all grow old like a garment; Like a cloak You will change them, And they will be changed. But You are the same, And Your years will have no end." (Psalm 102:26-27)

"He who does not love does not know God, for God is love." (1 John 4:8)

"Jesus Christ is the same yesterday, today, and forever." (Hebrews 13:8)

XII

A SECURE BORDER
(BORDER WALL)

Satan Appears as an Angel of Light: We need a world in which people are free to live and work wherever they please. No person is illegal.

Satan's Goal: Protect criminals and evil that harm the innocent. Destruction of a country that promotes liberty and freedom to preach the Gospel.

What does the Bible say?
"So the wall was finished on the twenty-fifth day of Elul, in fifty-two days. And it happened, when all our enemies heard of it, and all the nations around us saw these things, that they were very disheartened in their own eyes; for they perceived that this work was done by our God." Nehemiah (6:15-16)

"For which of you, intending to build a tower, does not sit down first and count the cost, whether he has enough to finish it." (Luke 14:28)

Satan is never satisfied, he will find any way to oppose God and destroy… The Democrat Party's scheme of trading votes for government handouts has been exported beyond the borders of the United States. As a result, Democrats want to bring anyone (non-citizens) to America from foreign countries including criminals using numerous schemes, such as open borders, chain migration and the DREAM Act. To expand their base, secure power and trap more people in bondage, they want to trade government handouts for votes of non- citizens. There is a big movement today by Democrats to abolish ICE (Immigration and Customs Enforcement) and give illegals (non-citizens) the right to vote in American elections. The Democrat Party wants to let people from failed countries as well as enemy countries that have no understanding of the history or culture of America and allow them to vote. With this scheme, the Democrat Party is trading the security and liberty of U.S. citizens to obtain more votes. It is the reason that the Democrat Party platform supports open borders and no border wall.

It is not out of compassion or to help people. It is about trapping people on government handouts and that is not liberty, it is bondage. Most illegal immigrants that flow into America obtain some type of government handout. Secondly, to pay for all the government handouts to illegals flowing into America, it takes the liberty, prosperity and opportunity from the hard-working taxpayers and citizens.

Hillary Clinton said, "My dream is a hemispheric common market, with open trade and open borders."

Liberal musician Carlos Santana said, "One day there will be no borders, no boundaries, no flags and no countries and the only passport will be the heart."

In 2018, A Democratic gubernatorial candidate for Arizona asked an audience at a liberal event to imagine a future without a border wall. David Garcia said, "I want to just take a second and imagine. Let's just imagine … Just imagine no wall. No wall in southern Arizona." Mr. Garcia was met with applause and cheers from the liberal audience.

On face value the desire for open borders is fraudulent and nonsensical. Common sense dictates that you lock the doors of your home at night to protect your family and possessions. The president of the United States resides in the White House, surrounded by a fence with heavily armed guards on the roof and identification is required when you visit… Attempt to walk into a large call center of a business and you will be met by security guards at the entrance. Security guards will require that you show identification and cause for entry. Once verified, many visitors still require an escort before accessing the building, because they are not allowed to roam freely.

Conservative Republican Alan Keyes said, "When a country loses the will to defend its borders, when a country loses the will to assert its identity, when a country loses the will to stand in defense of its way of life, that country is doomed."

Republican President Ronald Reagan said, "A nation that cannot control its borders is not a nation."

The main reasons for a secure border or border wall are:
1. Deny criminals safe harbors
2. Deny America's enemies entry
3. Prevent an over burden on communities
4. Stop influx of illegal drugs
5. Protect businesses and consumers from counterfeit goods

Deny Criminals Safe Harbors
With open borders there would be no way to identify people who crossed into the country illegally. Individuals could cross the open border and commit acts such as robbery, rape and murder and then disappear back into another country. No one would know who they were or have any way to find them. Even if fingerprints were left behind, there would be no way to identify that criminal. America also would have no authority to go into another sovereign country to arrest the criminal. There would be no personal record or address of the criminal committing the crime, because the criminal is a citizen of another country. By creating open borders, you would be aiding, abetting criminals and evil in society.

America has Sworn Enemies.
America has sworn enemies that wish to do it harm. The history of the world is of wars between countries. Iran's parliament and their leaders chant, "Death to America", and ISIS posts videos threatening to destroy cities in America. There are also many Islamic countries that wish to see America destroyed. Let us not forget the terrorist attack on the World Trade Center on September 11, 2001. It is proof that evil wants to destroy America. There are also some countries,

like Russia and China that send spies to America to steal our secrets. No border security is an open door for terrorists to come into America to destroy it and for countries to steal our secrets.

Prevent an Over-Burden on Border Communities

Open borders would place tremendous burdens on communities along those borders. Roads, schools, infrastructure, housing, jobs, medical help, and financial aid would be stretched beyond capacity of those cities.

A Border Helps to Stop the Influx of Illegal Drugs

The majority of the illegal drugs come into the United States across the 2,000-mile border between the United States and Mexico. Without a secure border or border wall, highly addicting and deadly drugs would come unimpeded into America which would cause increases in drug addiction, homelessness and death. Remember, that is Satan's goal, to steal kill and destroy! The very same agenda of the Democrat Party, it is why they support open borders….

Protect Business Owners and Consumers from Counterfeit Goods

Not only are people, drugs and guns smuggled across the border, but fake designer products are as well. In 2018, in Laredo, Texas the U.S. Immigration and Customs Enforcement (ICE) uncovered 181,615 fake designer clothing and accessories worth an estimated $43 million dollars being smuggled into the America. The counterfeit items were meant to resemble Apple, Chanel, Coach, Gucci, Louis Vuitton, Nike and Sony… The items were substandard quality that would have taken profits from the real businesses and cheated consumers that thought they were getting the real thing. Once again, Democrats want to punish hard working individuals and businesses and reward lawlessness.

The Biblical Reasons for a Border Wall

Those reasons should merit a secure border, but this book is about exposing the fact that the Democrat Party platform is anti-Biblical. It is the Democrat Party that desires open borders, and this is not Biblical. I am going to provide two Biblical reasons in support of a border wall or a secure border for America.

Nehemiah Builds a Wall around Jerusalem

The first Biblical example for borders and a border wall is found in the book of Nehemiah. When King Nebuchadnezzar destroyed Jerusalem, he knocked down the walls and burned the gates of the city. It left the Israelites defenseless. With no walls, their enemies could easily enter the city plunder it and attack the people.

Nehemiah was told by his brother, *"The wall and gates surrounding the city are all fallen down. The people are in trouble."* Nehemiah then returned to Jerusalem. When he arrived, he looked over the city to see what needed to be done. He told the people he had returned and was going to rebuild the wall and gates. The wall was protection for the people and the gates were a method of allowing only certain people entry into the city. When the enemies of the Israelites heard the news that Nehemiah was going to rebuild the wall, they were determined to stop him. They also mocked Nehemiah for building the wall. If you do not believe that Democrats are against America, just look at their platform on a secure border and a border wall. Their tactics are on the same page with the enemies of Jerusalem at that time. The enemies of Jerusalem wanted to stop Nehemiah from building a wall to protect the city and Democrats are against a secure border or building a wall to protect America.

Nehemiah had a plan. During the day, while construction took place, he placed half the people to guard with weapons and the other half to build. At night, he placed people to guard the wall at various key defensive points. Nehemiah and the Israelites built the wall at the same time that they fought off their enemies. As a result, the wall was built in just 52 days.

The Bible says, *"So the wall was finished on the twenty-fifth day of Elul, in fifty-two days. And it happened, when all our enemies heard of it, and all the nations around us saw these things, that they were very disheartened in their own eyes; for they perceived that this work was done by our God."* (Nehemiah 6:15-16)

The Bible says when the enemies of the Israelites heard the news they were disheartened and sad, because they knew it was the work of God. The Democrat Party would be happy if the wall was not built and the borders of America not secure. They also would be disheartened if it was. It is the same emotion of the enemies of the Israelites that wanted to destroy Jerusalem….

I once listened to a pastor give a sermon on Nehemiah building the wall. He said that the people worked with one hand and fought with the other…. This is symbolic of a country protecting itself. Half the battle is fighting off the enemy and the other half is providing security.

The Second Biblical Example for a Secure Border: Count the Cost

Anytime that you plan to build something of value, whether it is a road, house or community you must count the cost. If you do not count the cost, you may not have the funds to finish it.

The Bible says, *"For which of you, intending to build a tower, does not sit down first and count the cost, whether he has enough to finish it— lest, after he has laid the foundation, and is not able to finish, all who see it begin to mock him, saying, 'This man began to build and was not able to finish'?"* (Luke 14:28-30)

In the scripture, Jesus was saying to count the cost for following Him. There is a cost to you if you are going to be a Believer. You need to count that cost and make sure you can pay it. Jesus used the example of building a tower. When you build a tower or a structure, count the cost to make sure that you have enough resources to finish it. A person would not want to begin building a $250,000 building, if they have only $5,000.

In Orlando Florida, there is a building (the Majesty Building) that was started in 2001. The cost was not counted and to this day (17 years later), the building remains unfished. As a result, it has been mocked citywide….

If you are going to build a city or a country, you must count the cost. Imagine the street next to your house is an open border and on the other side of that street is another country. Imagine there was no fence, no check points, no limitations and anyone could pass unrestricted between the two countries. Also imagine that your country was wealthy, had jobs and was a country of freedom. The country across the border was filled with corruption, crime and poverty…. There would be an influx of people into your town that would be overwhelming that you could not control. As I stated it would place an over burden on the communities along the border.

City Planning Commissions Count the Cost

Every city has a planning commission that counts the cost. The commission determines the number of police, schools, hospitals, businesses, roads and the housing needed based on the population. If there was an unlimited influx of people without controls, there would not be enough schools (overcrowded classrooms), not enough jobs (increased unemployment), not enough hospitals (shortage of medical treatment), not enough police to keep order (innocent people victimized), not enough housing (raising the cost of living accommodations) and not enough roads (causing traffic congestion). There would be also an increasing burden on the taxpayer to pay for all the people crossing the open border. It would chaos and disorder… The citizens doing the right things, working and providing for their families and community services would carry the burden and be penalized.

The Tactics of the Democrat Party

As I mentioned, one of the tactics of the Democrat Party is to silence their opposition. Remember, if you are not with God, you are against Him. What do Democrats do to those that oppose open borders? They call their opposition racist and they make the false argument that their opponents do not want immigration. Just as the wall in Jerusalem had gates to only allow certain individuals in the city that meant no harm. Proponents of secure borders for America desire the same. They want regulated immigration. They want to allow people into America that mean no harm to the country and in a regulated number that does not diminish the services that are provided to its citizens.

The Hypocrisy of Democrats

No border security or a border wall leaves you defenseless to those that wish to do you harm. Those that propose open borders are hypocrites. They live in homes with walls, gates, security and locks on their doors. They make sure they and their families are safe. The average citizen cannot afford walls or security around their homes. You will also not see illegal immigrants from other countries invited into their wealthy communities and they do not invite them to live in their homes.

Native American Indians had no Borders

Native American Indians in North America had no border, no walls around a city and no walls around their homes. They were totally defenseless to invasion. What happened to the Native American Indian? They were conquered! The Democrat Party points to the Native American Indian as a group of people that genocide was committed against, but that is how Democrats want to America to model their borders after.

Separating Children from Parents

I want to address separating children from their parents when it comes to immigration. Democrats and the liberal media have made this a big issue and portrayed those enforcing the border as mean and evil because parents that come across the border with their children illegally sometimes are separated when they are caught. If a parent and child are illegal and attempt to cross the border illegally, it is breaking the law. As a result, the parent and child do get separated. A child should not be held in a facility with criminal adults where they could be preyed upon. The same happens to a person committing a crime in America and gets arrested. Parent and child are separated. The child is not placed in a prison with the parent… Please be aware that individuals who serve in the military and are deployed into service are separated from their families for extended periods of time. Lastly, do you know where there is a wall, gates and an extreme vetting process where parents are separated from their children? It is Heaven.

The Bible says, *"Also she had a great and high wall with twelve gates, and twelve angels at the gates, and names written on them, which are the names of the twelve tribes of the children of Israel: three gates on the east, three gates on the north, three gates on the south, and three gates on the west. Now the wall of the city had twelve foundations, and on them were the names of the twelve apostles of the Lamb. And he who talked with me had a gold reed to measure the city, its gates, and its wall."* (Revelation 21:12-15)

Why does heaven need walls and a gate? Heaven is an exclusive place that cannot be entered by the wicked and evil that are not worthy.

The Bible says, *"Blessed are those who do His commandments, that they may have the right to the tree of life, and may enter through the gates into the city. But outside are dogs and sorcerers and sexually immoral and murderers and idolaters, and whoever loves and practices a lie."* (Revelation 22:14-15)

XIII

AMERICA FIRST

Satan Appears as an Angel of Light: America First is racist and divisive. American unilateralism is putting world economic growth at risk and alienates American allies. It leaves America isolated and disadvantaged in the world.

Satan's Goal: Weaken or destroy a country founded on Christian principles and liberty. Enable and become partners with discrimination, bondage, evil and tyranny. Also assist other countries that mean harm to America.

What does the Bible say? *"One who rules his own house well, having his children in submission with all reverence (for if a man does not know how to rule his own house, how will he take care of the church of God?)"* (1 Timothy 3:4)

"America First" was one of the slogans of Republican President Donald Trump when he ran for president in 2016. It is a reference to putting America's priorities as a country over foreign countries and putting the needs of American citizens above non-citizens. There was much controversy about this slogan, especially from the Democrat Party and liberals who said it was racist, divisive and alienates America from allies. This accusation coming from an organization that survives on identity politics.

You Place your Families' Needs above your Neighbors

On face value, putting your own country over other foreign countries is common sense. Once again, the Democrat Party lies and deceives. Placing your country first does not mean completely alienating your allies. It means creating order and that your own country comes first. Shouldn't you shelter and feed your own children before you shelter and feed someone else's children? It would be illogical to live in a homeless shelter, while you pay the expenses of another family to live. You place your own family's needs above your neighbors, yet they are still your friends. I have had close friends my entire my life, even before I became a Christian, yet my family always came first. It would be inappropriate to do otherwise. My Christian friends that I have now, I can count on dearly, yet I place my family above them... I would never expect any of them to place me above their own families. It would be disrespectful, inappropriate and an insult to my family to place my neighbor's wife and children above my own.

Where to Rank your Country?

If you do not put your own country first in terms of importance, where do you place it with respect to other countries? How do you rank your own country in terms of its needs and the needs of your own people related to other countries? Do you put some countries ahead of your own and not others? If that is your belief, what criteria do you use? Do you put your allies ahead of your own country and not countries that you consider to be enemies? Do you put all countries ahead of your own including enemy countries? During World War II should America put Germany's needs above its own? What about countries that are neutral to America, but engage in human rights abuses and genocide, do you put their needs above those of America and Americans?

Let's start with placing the needs of an enemy country above the needs of America. Some of these countries desire the destruction of America such as Iran. As a result, do we fund their armies over our own army? Many of our enemies are countries led by dictators. As I stated previously, when you give funds to dictators, the funds do not go to the people, but to the dictator's lavish lifestyle and to strengthen the dictators rule over the country. By supporting dictatorships over America, it is taking away from the citizens of America and helping to oppress people trapped in a dictatorship. Also, many countries that consider themselves enemies of America fund terrorism across the world. If we give these countries funds and support them, aren't we helping to enable terrorism? Aren't we then accessories?

There are some countries that are neutral to the United States that jail people for political speech, deny women basic rights, engage in ethnic cleansing and will put you to death or imprison you for preaching the Gospel. Yet, the Bible tells us to preach the Gospel to every creature. Are we to put these countries needs ahead of our own? To place those countries in importance ahead of America, is foolishness. It is supporting evil and is a recipe for destruction of your America. The Bible says we are to not have any relationship with evil and we should expose it.

The Bible says, *"And have no fellowship with the unfruitful works of darkness, but rather expose them."* (Ephesians 5:11)

The definition of fellowship is company of equals or friends. We should have no (zero) companionship with those who are engaged in evil and we should expose it. If you know someone is a child molester or abuses women, would you befriend that person, help them and financially support them? Of course not! However, that is just what the Democrat Party is in saying when they come against an "America First" agenda. They are saying befriend, help and financially support other countries above America, even those committing atrocities, genocide or engaging in human rights abuses.

Do not be Unequally Yoked

When I dedicated myself to the Lord, I had built up friendships that had lasted decades…. My values when I dedicated myself to the Lord, however, had changed. My friends' values and the things I used to do with them did not interest me any longer. I was a new creation in Christ.

The Bible says, "Therefore, if anyone is in Christ, he is a new creation; old things have passed away; behold, all things have become new." (2 Corinthians 5:17)

Let me give you an example… Before I was saved, when I saw a homeless man, I had no compassion. I would think, "he did that to himself and better him than me." After I got saved and learned the word of God, I gained compassion and understanding. Now I think, "that poor man, Satan got to him, how can I help him?" I invited my friends to church, but they were not interested. I tried to keep them in my life, but our priorities were different. I was seeking God and they were seeking the world. If they did not want to follow Jesus with me, I had to leave them behind. I had to separate myself from them and that is what I did.

The Bible says, *"Do not be unequally yoked together with unbelievers. For what fellowship has righteousness with lawlessness? And what [communion has light with darkness? And what accord has Christ with Belial? Or what part has a believer with an unbeliever? And what agreement has the temple of God with idols? For you are the temple of the living God. As God has said: "I will dwell in them And walk among them. I will be their God, And they shall be My people." Therefore "Come out from among them And be separate, says the Lord. Do not touch what is unclean, And I will receive you." "I will be a Father to you, And you shall be My sons and daughters, Says the Lord Almighty."* (2 Corinthians 6:14-18)

God is a God of Order

If you look at the story of creation, God created the universe in perfect order. God created light and water before plants. If this was not the case, the plants would have died. God created plants before animals, if this were not so, the animals would have no food to eat and die. God is perfect, and His order is perfect.

Scientists have been able to understand the properties of the universe through mathematical equations. The laws of the universe, such as the movement of light, planets, galaxies and gravity are determined by mathematical formulas. When solving complicated mathematical equations, they must be solved in specific order and if done out of order, the answer is incorrect. This is true even for an equation as simple as $3(2 + 3) \times 2 = 30$. The addition of $2 + 3$ within parenthesis must be added before it is multiplied by 3 or the answer is wrong.

The first commandment is to "have no other Gods before me". God puts Himself first for a reason. If God is not first in your life then everything in your life will be out of order. If you put friendships, work, television, recreation or money first in your life over God, that will become a god to you and rule over you.

Within the family, God creates an order. God again is always first.

Next, although man and woman are equal, man is the head. If the wife rules the house, the house is out of order. I once knew a couple where the woman ruled the house and she placed her grown children above her husband. She said, "she gave birth to her children and her husband could leave and divorce her." As a result, the husband was diminished within the home. The wife had an emotional bond, because of childbirth and she could not let go of that bond even though the children were in their thirties. She let emotion rule over reason, because of the bond of childbirth. It is one of the reasons that God placed the man as the head. The entire house was out of order with the children having authority over the husband.

In some families, the children rule over the parents. Imagine that? What do you think happens in these families? Children do not have the best interest of the entire family in mind, but their own. They know nothing of finances, taxes or paying bills. How can they rule over a home? It would create even more chaos and disorder. If you look at many single-family homes where there is no father, the children have too much authority and as a result, the homes are in chaos.

Democrats Twist the Word of God

To argue against "America First", Democrats cite the scriptures *"Love your neighbor as yourself"*, to *"help the least of these"* or point to the parable of the Good Samaritan. These scriptures are instructions for how Christians are to treat others. Yes, we are to do these things as Christians, but before we do these things we have to care for our own families. There is nothing in these scriptures about placing other countries above your own or other families above your own. At the start of this chapter, I stated that it is logical to place your own family first before that of a neighbor's. The Bible is specific that you take care of your own family first. The Bible says there must be order in your own home first before you can serve in the church. Anyone who wants to serve in the church, their household must be in order first. If your own house is not in order, how can you serve God? It is an example that your own home comes first.

The Bible says, *"one who rules his own house well, having his children in submission with all reverence (for if a man does not know how to rule his own house, how will he take care of the church of God?)"* (1 Timothy 3:4)

Lastly, the Bible says that you must take care of your own family or you are worse than an unbeliever. Amazing, the Democrat Party does not want you to take care of your own, but instead take care of others first and that is not Biblical. Yes, we are to help others, but we must have our own house in order take care of our own family first.

The Bible says, *"But if anyone does not provide for his own, and especially for those of his household, he has denied the faith and is worse than an unbeliever."*

America First is Biblical!

The Pursuit of Happiness

XIV

HOMOSEXUALITY AND GAY MARRIAGE

Satan Appears as an Angel of Light. There is nothing wrong when two people love each other even if they are the same sex. Love is beautiful. It should be legal for gay, lesbian, bisexual and transgender individuals to marry to ensure equal rights for all.

Satan's Goal: The destruction of the family and ultimately society, because if you destroy the family, you destroy society.

What does the Bible say?
"You shall not lie with a male as with a woman. It is an abomination." (Leviticus 18:22)

"Do you not know that the unrighteous will not inherit the kingdom of God? Do not be deceived. Neither fornicators, nor idolaters, nor adulterers, nor homosexuals, nor sodomites, nor thieves, nor covetous, nor drunkards, nor revilers, nor extortioners will inherit the kingdom of God." (1 Corinthians 6:9)

I placed the topic of homosexuality in the section of Happiness, because the Democrat Party believes happiness can be achieved chasing selfish immoral desires of the flesh. That is a lie from Satan tempting you with the lust of the flesh to be disobedient to the word of God. Once you have spent some time on this earth, you will know that chasing desires of the flesh will not bring happiness. It only leads to sorrow, regret, heartache and destruction.

My many years before I dedicated myself to the Lord was spent chasing the things of the world. I did not know the word of God, so I lived according to the world's standards. The world said, you are judged by how pretty your wife is, the car you drive, the house you live in and the amount of money that you make. It was the lust of the flesh, the lust of the eyes and the pride of life. That is what I chased… It never led to happiness. It led me down a path of emptiness, stress, financial problems and wasted time.

The Democrat Party is in support of homosexuality and gay marriage and both positions are not Biblical. They believe it is the right of every person to have a sexual relationship with anyone they choose. They consider it love. They also support gay marriage and say it is discrimination if two people of the same sex cannot marry. They do not stop there. If you express a Biblical view in opposition to what they say, you will be labeled a homophobe. The definition of homophobe is a person who hates or is afraid of homosexuals or treats them badly.

Democrat Barack Obama said in reference to gay marriage, "love is love."

Accepting his Oscar for portraying gay rights activist Harvey Milk, Sean Penn said, "I think that it is a good time for those who voted for the ban against gay marriage to sit and reflect and anticipate their great shame and the shame in their grandchildren's eyes if they continue that way of support. We've got to have equal rights for everyone."

Actress Drew Barrymore said, "No one has any right to tell anyone what makes a family."

Democrat Nancy Pelosi on gay marriage said, "My religion has, compels me—and I love it for it—to be against discrimination of any kind in our country, and I consider [the ban on gay marriage] a form of discrimination."

Despite what Democrats and liberals say, Christians are not homophobes. It is just another lie. There is an old Christian saying, "love the sinner, but hate the sin." Horatius Bonar said, "God's hatred of the sin is not hatred of the sinner." The truth is that God loves you! He sent His Son to die for you, to take away your sins.

Billy Graham said, "God proved His love on the Cross. When Christ hung, and bled, and died, it was God saying to the world, I love you."

The Bible says, *"For God so loved the world that He gave His only begotten Son, that whoever believes in Him should not perish but have everlasting life. For God did not send His Son into the world to condemn the world, but that the world through Him might be saved."* (John 3:16-17)

God wants you to turn from your sin. If you steal, you are to stop stealing. If you lie, you are to stop lying and so on. Christians love everyone and it is the reason why they want people to turn from sin. If Christians hated homosexuals, they would tell them to keep on sinning. Actually, that is exactly what the Democrat Party does… The word of God is clear on the issue of homosexuality, and God says that it is a sin.

The Old Testament calls homosexuality an abomination. An abomination is a strong word. It means offensive or opposing to the things of God. If something is an abomination to God, it is rejected and not embraced by God. If you support something that God opposes, you are against the will of God. You are saying, "God, you are wrong, and I am smarter than you." That is arrogant and prideful. Remember Satan was cast from heaven for pride, for wanting to elevate himself above God. When you believe you are right, and God is wrong, you are elevating yourself above God. Joel Osteen said, "Don't put a question mark where God has put a period."

The New Testament in First Corinthians gives a list of sins that is warned against by God that will result in not getting to heaven. These sins are fornication, idolatry, adultery, homosexuality, sodomy, stealing, coveting, drunkenness, extortion and being abusive. The scripture states that homosexuals will not inherit the kingdom of God (heaven). Homosexuality is a sin and yes, we are all sinners. But we are to turn from our sin and repent, not endorse it. There is a vast difference between committing sin and then repenting and the continual non-repentance and endorsement of sin. If you are going to endorse homosexuality, you may as well endorse fornication, idolatry, adultery, sodomy, stealing drunkenness, extortion and abuse....

The Bible says that the qualification for forgiveness of sin is repentance. Repentance is to feel sorrow, regret or contrition for sin. It is to change one's mind in relation to a sin. To gain forgiveness from God, you must ask God for forgiveness with a repentant heart. If you have an extra marital affair that is adultery. Unless you are truly sorrowful for your actions and ask God for forgiveness you are not repenting. When you support or endorse sin, there is no repentance. It is saying that the sin is okay. Supporting gay marriage is an endorsement of homosexuality (sin) and endorsing is the opposite of repentance.

Billy Sunday "A sinner has no standing with God. He forfeits his standing when he commits sin and the only way he can get back is to repent and accept the atoning blood of Jesus Christ."

Charles Finney said, "The Bible teaches that sin is forgiven when it is repented of, but never while it is persisted in."

Franklin Graham said this about homosexuality, "But the gay person is going to have to repent of their sins and turn from their sins, leave their sins."

The Bible says, *"Repent therefore and be converted, that your sins may be blotted out, so that times of refreshing may come from the presence of the Lord."* (Acts 3:19)

Repent and God will Forgive you
Whatever your sin, if you repent and ask God for forgiveness, He will forgive you. God is our father in heaven. If your child made a mistake and came to you truly sorry about something he or she had done, wouldn't you forgive that child? If you say no, well God is perfect, and His forgiveness is perfect.

Today, there are many Christians who support homosexuality and gay marriage. They either do not know the word of God or they are consciously opposing it. I once heard a Christian woman talking about going to a drag show (men dressed as women). She stated, "I do not think there is anything in the Bible that says it is wrong." She was wrong! She is lacking Biblical knowledge. The Bible is so clear on the topic of homosexuality that is says that men should not even dress as woman and women not dress as men.

The Bible says, *"A woman shall not wear anything that pertains to a man, nor shall a man put on a woman's garment, for all who do so are an abomination to the Lord your God."* (Deuteronomy 22:5)

Cross dressing (wear clothing typical of the opposite sex), is an abomination to God. Again, an abomination means offensive or opposing to the things of God.

Also, today there are some pastors who support homosexuality and gay marriage. I am not sure what Bible they are reading? Again, if you endorse homosexuality, you also must endorse those other sins listed in First Corinthians. Can you imagine hearing a sermon from that church? It would have to go something like this…. it is okay to steal, have sex outside of marriage, have gay sex, get drunk, steal and abuse people…. Sounds like the church of Satan!

God's position on homosexuality in the Old Testament and New Testament is clear. Sodom and Gomorrah give even greater insight into God's stance on homosexuality. The sin of homosexuality was part of the reason these two cities were destroyed by God. Men of Sodom and Gomorrah wanted to perform homosexual rape on the two angels (who were disguised as men). That is how the word sodomy came to be used to refer to anal sex.

The Bible says, *"as Sodom and Gomorrah, and the cities around them in a similar manner to these, having given themselves over to sexual immorality and gone after strange flesh, are set forth as an example, suffering the vengeance of eternal fire."* (Jude 1:7)

Satan Wants to Silence You

Again, a tactic of the Democrat Party is to silence you and keep you on the sidelines. If you oppose gay marriage, they label you as intolerant or a homophobe. Unless you know the word of God, you could fall for that tactic. Remember, you are either with God or against God. I stand firm in my opposition to gay marriage. Supporting gay marriage endorses the homosexual lifestyle. The Bible says we are to warn others of their sin, not endorse it or God will hold us accountable. I stand with God. God is bigger than any Democrat or any liberal celebrity. The words of Fatty Arbuckle (actor), Chester Arthur (president), Edward R. Murrow (News broadcaster) are all forgotten, but the Words of the Bible have carried on for thousands of years. I will put my trust in God

You cannot support parts of God's word and not other parts. You cannot pick and choose. The Bible is all true or none of it is true. To pick and choose what you want to believe is saying that you are wiser than God. Again, to think you are smarter than God is arrogance and pride and God warns against it.

The Bible says, "Woe to *those who are* wise in their own eyes, And prudent in their own sight!" (Isaiah 5:21)

Moral Equivalency

The Bible is the moral authority for Christians. Without a moral authority, morality would be on a case by case basis. What is moral for one person, would not be moral for another. You cannot ignore the slippery slope of Satan. We have seen as time goes that man's standards change with time. God's standards never change. We see today people wanting to marry their computer, sex dolls and robots. Are pets going to be next? There are stories in the news where people are having sexual relations with animals. What does the Bible say about sexual relations with other living things? The Bible says:

"Whoever lies with an animal shall surely be put to death." (Exodus 22:19)

"Nor shall you mate with any animal, to defile yourself with it. Nor shall any woman stand before an animal to mate with it. It is perversion." (Leviticus 18:23)

The Bible says sexual relations with animals is perversion. Again, perversion is the alteration of something from its original course and meaning, or corruption of what was first intended. Satan perverts' things meant for good and turning them from their original intention to destroy. It is exactly what the Democrat Party does. This entire book is about the Democrat Party perverting the word of God to destroy. Let me give you an example... The Boy Scouts of America was founded in 1910. Recently, bowing to pressure from Democrats, liberals and the LGBT community, they allowed openly gay scouts and scout leaders to join their program. They then changed their name to Scouts BSA and began to allow girls into their ranks. After such decisions and many lawsuits, they filed bankruptcy in 2018.

Lastly, the Bible only speaks of marriage between man (husband) and woman (wife).   The definition of a wife is a married woman considered in relation to her spouse. A husband is defined as a married man considered in relation to his spouse.

The Bible says, *"And Adam said: 'This is now bone of my bones And flesh of my flesh; She shall be called Woman, Because she was taken out of Man.' Therefore a man shall leave his father and mother and be joined to his wife, and they shall become one flesh."* (Genesis 2:23–24)

Today, there are gender neutral pronouns to replace male and female. There is Ey, Ne, Xe, Ze…. Currently, Democrats and liberals have come up with hundreds of ways to self-identify beyond male and female. The Democrat Party is in support of people defining themselves as whatever they want to be. If you are a man, you can say that you are a female. If you are a female, you can say that you are male. You can also be gender fluid. They say God made a mistake. God never makes mistakes.

The Bible says, *"Therefore, beloved, looking forward to these things, be diligent to be found by Him in peace, without spot and blameless; and consider that the longsuffering of our Lord is salvation—as also our beloved brother Paul, according to the wisdom given to him, has written to you, as also in all his epistles, speaking in them of these things, in which are some things hard to understand, which untaught and unstable people twist to their own destruction, as they do also the rest of the Scriptures."* (2 Peter 3:14-16)

The Democrat Party is so opposed to the word of God, they are against Christian counseling on homosexuality. They are currently enacting laws making it illegal to counsel homosexuals and warning that it is a sin. I know of many men and women that lived homosexual lifestyles, but when they learned of the word of God, turned from homosexuality. One young man told me after turning from the homosexual lifestyle, that he felt lied to by the world his entire life. He now is happily married and has a child.

Turning from homosexuality is not the desire of Satan or the Democrat Party. Once again, the Democrat platform is the same as Satan's of endorsing sin. They try to silence you and enact laws that prevent people from learning the truth about the word of God. They do not want you to repent, because repentance is the first step to forgiveness which leads to salvation.

God wants you to repent and to ask for forgiveness. Leonard Ravenhill said, "No vice, however horrendous, will keep us out of Heaven if repented of. No virtue, however admirable, will get us into Heaven without the blood of Christ." God wants all to accept Jesus as their savior in their heart and to turn from sin. God does not want anyone to perish. God wants all of us to live with Him in heaven.

The Bible says, *"The Lord is not slack concerning His promise, as some count slackness, but is longsuffering toward us, not willing that any should perish but that all should come to repentance."* (2 Peter 3:9)

XV

EVIRONMENTALISM
(GLOBAL WARMING/ CLIMATE CHANGE)

Satan Appears as an Angle of Light: Human activity is responsible for global climate change. Climate change poses an urgent threat to the environment, wildlife, economies, national security and the health and well-being of people.

Satan's Goal: Create worship of a false god to create chaos, halt progress, punish success and destroy lives.

What does the Bible say? *"Then God blessed them, and God said to them, "Be fruitful and multiply; fill the earth and subdue it; have dominion over the fish of the sea, over the birds of the air, and over every living thing that moves on the earth."* (Genesis 1:28)

It was first called "global warming" by environmentalists. Liberals and the Democrat Party claimed that the earth was warming due to human activity, specifically in developed countries. Al Gore made a movie about it in 2006 called, "An Inconvenient Truth", which made a lot of predictions about global warming. However, as the years passed harsh winters, record snow and record cold temperatures continually occurred. The predictions of climate scientists and Al Gore were wrong. They were not wrong by a little, but by a lot. Rush Limbaugh once debated Al Gore on climate change long before his movie in 2006. Every prediction from that debate by Al Gore failed to materialize. In fact, all of Al Gore's predictions from his movie, failed to materialize. The only thing his environmental campaign accomplished was make him a great deal of money and win him a

151

Nobel Peace Prize. It also indoctrinated a lot of young people into environmentalism.

When none of the predictions of the dire consequences of global warming materialized, the Democrat Party changed "global warming" to "climate change". What does that mean? It means that there is going to be a change in global or regional climate patterns. No kidding, everything changes over time… However, climate alarmists say it is attributed to the increased levels of atmospheric carbon dioxide produced using fossil fuels. If you look at the history of the earth. The climate changed even before man appeared upon it.

Democrat Barrack Obama said, "No challenge poses a greater threat to future generations than climate change."

Democrat Bernie Sanders said, "The scientific community is telling us that if we do not address the global crisis of climate change, transform our energy system away from fossil fuel to sustainable energy, the planet that we're going to be leaving our kids and our grandchildren may well not be habitable."

Actress Natalie Portman said, "We do to God's creatures what the Nazis did to us… As long as people will shed the blood of innocent creatures there can be no peace, no liberty, no harmony. Slaughter and justice cannot dwell together."

I am not going to debate the scientific facts over what is now called climate change. Thousands of scientists disagree whether the earth's climate is cooling or getting warmer. Also, thousands of scientists disagree whether climate change is due to human activity. To debate scientific arguments is pointless, because so many experts disagree, and you would not be able to determine what is true or not. People make mistakes and scientists can lie. Let me give you some common-sense wisdom from Rush Limbaugh. In refuting the climate change scheme, he said that it is folly that scientists who cannot determine the path of a hurricane, a prediction of hours or days, then want to claim they can determine what the temperature of the earth will be 50 years. He is right!

Climate Change is the Entire Liberal Agenda in one Lie
The Democrat Party engages in worshiping false gods, punishing

success, taking away freedoms and destroying lives and it is all wrapped up in the single issue of climate change.

Worshiping a False God

The Democrat Party will do anything to stop you from worshipping God. Their goal is for you to worship them, but if they cannot do that, they will try to make you worship anything else but God. There is something called Gaia Worship. It is the uniting of all life forms around the goddess of Mother Earth. It is nature worship. People really believe this stuff. You may think this is extreme, but Democrats and liberals have created something called Earth Day. This is a day to celebrate the earth. These are the same people who turn Christmas, the celebration of the birth Jesus Christ into Santa Clause and happy holidays!

I took a ride to the beach one early evening with my wife. We enjoy the beach at night. We usually take two chairs, popcorn and some water and just sit at the edge of the ocean. We listen to the sound of the ocean and look at the stars in the night. God's creation is wonderous and far more glorious than watching any movie starring liberal actors that are actively opposing the word of God.

The Bible says, *"The heavens declare the glory of God; And the firmament shows His handiwork."*

One evening, while my wife and I were sitting in our chairs at the beach, a young man was doing some type of exercise on the edge of the ocean. When he was done, he bowed to the ocean and walked away. Bowing is bending the head or body or knee as a sign of reverence or submission. This young man was submitting himself to the ocean.

The Bible says, *"In the beginning God created the heavens and the earth."* (Genesis 1:1)

The young man, instead of worshipping God was worshipping the ocean. He was worshipping what God created instead of God.

Punishing Success and Halting Progress

Again, the Democrat Party always punishes success and rewards failure. I demonstrated that in the chapter regarding the progressive income tax. With environmentalism, the Democrat Party also punishes success and rewards failure. They believe poor undeveloped countries are victims and need compensation from wealthy advanced countries. They believe that wealthy countries must be punished for their success. As a result, wealth is taken from the rich and given to the poor. On local levels, businesses must be punished in favor of the environment and animals.

The Paris Climate Treaty was an agreement between numerous countries to regularly report on the contribution that each undertakes to mitigate global warming. The agreement required that developed nations help developing countries with the costs of going green, and the costs of coping with the effects of climate change. However, the targets for each country were not legally binding and a country is not penalized if they fail to meet their target. There is also no guarantee that the agreement would have any impact on the climate. What does this mean? It means developed countries are going to pay a lot of money (wealth transfer) to poor mismanaged and corrupt countries, because of an agreement that is not binding and has no impact.

When Republican Donald Trump was elected president, he withdrew from the agreement. Trump stated, "The United States will withdraw from the Paris climate accord...I was elected to represent the citizens of Pittsburgh, not Paris." Trump also said, "This agreement is less about the climate and more about other countries gaining a financial advantage over the United States."

Environmentalism Halts Progress on National and Local Levels

There are endless examples of environmentalists attempting to stop progress in the name of environmentalism. The Keystone Pipeline is an oil pipeline system between Canada and the United States. It was held up by the Obama Administration for years, because Obama believed it would undercut United States leadership on reducing carbon admissions. Obama placed America's needs and priorities second to other countries. It was not until Republican Donald Trump became president that permits were granted, and the Keystone Pipeline was built.

On a local level, the Braken Bat Cave spider stopped a $15 million Texas highway construction project. The spider was more important than progress and enhancing the lives of people by reducing traffic.

More than 99 percent of all species that ever lived on Earth are estimated to be extinct. Everything lives, dies and new species are born. That is life on this planet. To put animals above humans is putting your cat or dog above you…

Taking Away Freedoms

The Democrat Party wants to limit your freedoms and prosperity in the name of the environment. One solution to their so-called climate crises is micro-houses. It is the tiny house movement. The Democrat Party believes in these tiny homes to save the environment. Tiny homes with very little space use less energy, this is true. However, studies show that there are higher rates of stress, substance abuse and domestic violence linked to tight living quarters. I learned this many years ago when I was in college at the age of 18. I lived in an apartment that was small, very small. It was a two-room apartment, made for poor college students. It had a living room and a small kitchen, which was an offshoot of that room. It also had one large bedroom with two beds. My roommate was a very nice person, but he drove me crazy, because we shared such a small space. When my roommate ate, I could hear every single bite he took. When he talked on the phone, there was no quiet or privacy. After a few months, I could not take it and would go outside and sit in my car to study…

Destroying Lives

Another idea from the Democrat Party to combat the climate crises is to legislate fuel efficient cars. These cars are very small. This is proof positive that the Democrat Party places animals above the lives of people. What is the problem with tiny cars? They are very unsafe! In 2012, President Barack Obama finalized standards increasing fuel economy to the equivalent of 54.5 mpg for cars and light-duty trucks by the model year 2025. Sounds great doesn't it? Fuel efficient cars for everyone… It is not great! The Democrat Party favors producing high mileage vehicles over the safety of you and your family. Have you seen some of these cars? They almost look like toys. I would not want to be on the highway in one and get in an accident. I am certain that you would not be in one of these vehicles with your children. Democrats do not favor drilling for oil in the Arctic (areas of vast nothingness), because it might hurt a caribou, but they have no issue with you driving a car so small that if you get into an accident, it will injure or kill you and your family. When

Republican Donald Trump became president, he reversed the mileage rules by Obama.

The Hypocrisy of Democrats

As I noted previously, all the schemes of the Democrat do not apply to them… They proclaim small houses, fuel efficiency and not disturbing the environment. However, the leaders of the Democrat Party and Hollywood liberals live in big houses, drive big SUV's or travel in private gas guzzling planes. Barbara Streisand, Al Gore, Leo DiCaprio, John Kerry, Bill Clinton, Democrat politicians and liberal celebrities do not live in tiny houses, but large mansions where the monthly electric bills are the equivalent to the average person's mortgage. And many of them have more than one mansion… it is hypocrisy.

What Does the Bible say?

Once again, the Democrat Party twists the word of God. They take what God means for good and pervert it. Environmentalism is no different. The Democrat definition of environmentalism is idolatry of the earth. It is turning the earth into a god. The earth is not to be worshiped. God is to be worshiped.

The Bible says, *"Then God blessed them, and God said to them, "Be fruitful and multiply; fill the earth and subdue it; have dominion over the fish of the sea, over the birds of the air, and over every living thing that moves on the earth."* (Genesis 1:28)

The Bible says that humans are to subdue the earth and have dominion over every living thing. The word subdue means to bring under subjection. The earth is to be under the subjection of humans and not the other way around. The word dominion means to have authority over. The Bible says that humans have authority over every living thing. However, the Democrat Party believes humans are to be under subjection and authority of the earth.

After creating Adam, the Bible says, *"The Lord God took the man and put him in the Garden of Eden to work it and take care of it"* (Genesis 2:15).

The Bible says that the earth is to be cared for by us. We are accountable to God for how we use it. God did not tell Adam to worship the earth. He did not tell Adam to exploit the earth or treat it recklessly, but to watch over it and use it wisely. If you plant a garden in your backyard, you do not worship it, you care for it and tend it. We are to work and care for the earth, but not let it rule over us. I have heard Democrats and liberals argue that the earth is overpopulated, and a plan is needed save the earth's resources. In fact, I once debated a liberal who believed that all people should die at a certain age to save animals and the earth's resources. This is entirely contradictory to the word of God.

XVI

SANCTUARY CITIES

Satan Appears as an Angel of Light: Sanctuary cities in America are needed to protect undocumented people against federal immigration laws. No one is illegal, and people need a safe harbor against persecution.

Satan's Goal: Create chaos in society. Protect criminals and allow them to inflict damage on society and to the innocent citizens.

What does the Bible say? *"then you shall appoint cities to be cities of refuge for you, that the manslayer who kills any person accidentally may flee there. They shall be cities of refuge for you from the avenger, that the manslayer may not die until he stands before the congregation in judgment."* (Numbers 35:11-12)

This is a separate issue than secure borders or a border wall. If there is a border wall, there will still be breaches and there would be sanctuary cities created and endorsed by the Democrat Party. There is no official definition of a sanctuary city. It refers to a city or county that protects illegal immigrants (even if they are criminals) by not cooperating with federal immigration authorities. Sanctuary cities defy federal laws to which state and local governments are legally bound.

The Democrat Party is in rebellion against authority and endorsing chaos. There is protocol in every organization and this includes everything from private business, public schools, private schools, states, counties, cities, and homeowner associations… You cannot have a secretary with authority over the CEO of a company. You cannot have a student with authority over a teacher. You cannot have a state public school teacher with authority over a governor. State law cannot be above federal law. If a state law does not fall within the guidelines of the federal law, it is illegal. Example: If a state decides to enact a law that supports discrimination, it violates federal law and it is illegal. You cannot have the federal government submitting to the state. You must understand that Satan rebelled against God. This is exactly what the Democrat Party is doing. They are rebelling against rightful authority and creating lawlessness.

The United States Federal Supreme Court is the ultimate authority on whether a state law is legal. Its decisions are based on whether a law or and action violates the United States Constitution. If a state enacted a law that required all women be paid less than men, a person who felt the law violated their rights could sue and take the case to a state court. Whatever the state court ruled in reference to the case, could be appealed all the way to the United States Federal Supreme Court. The Supreme Court has ultimate authority to determine whether the state law violated the Constitution.

Once the federal Supreme Court rules, states not complying with federal law regarding immigration are violating federal law. They are placing themselves above federal law and basically saying that they can do as they please. These Democrat Party leaders are subverting the law, justice and committing chaos intentionally. The sanctuary cities are harboring (protecting) criminals and that is illegal. If you harbored a criminal in your house, you would be guilty of a crime and go to jail.

What does the Bible say?
The Democrat Party once again twists the word of God to defend their schemes that rebel against authority, defend criminals and create chaos in society. They cite the correct scripture, but it is completely out of complex.

The Bible says, *"then you shall appoint cities to be cities of refuge for you, that the manslayer who kills any person accidentally may flee there. They shall be cities of refuge for you from the avenger, that the manslayer may not die until he stands before the congregation in judgment. And of the cities which you give, you shall have six cities of refuge. You shall appoint three cities on this side of the Jordan, and three cities you shall appoint in the land of Canaan, which will be cities of refuge. These six cities shall be for refuge for the children of Israel, for the stranger, and for the sojourner among them, that anyone who kills a person accidentally may flee there."* (Numbers 35:11-15)

The Bible is against murder. As I noted in the chapter on abortion, murder is the killing of an innocent person. However, if an altercation occurs between two people and one dies, it is not always clear if it is murder, self-defense or an accident. The Bible states at that time certain cities were designated as sanctuaries for individuals to flee to that were involved in such altercations, where the circumstances of death were not clear. It was done to protect the accused against vigilante justice. It was done so that the accused could get a fair trial.

If you continue to read the scripture in Numbers 35, it states that there are no sanctuary cities or any safe harbor for murderers. Those who intentionally committed murder were put to death. The sanctuary cities were created for circumstances that were unclear. In those circumstances, the accused went to the sanctuary cities to have their case go before the community to determine if the death was intentional or not. The accused was not automatically guilty or set free. The accused was held accountable. It was done to seek justice.

In Democrat sanctuary cities there are no trials so there is no justice. Criminals are not held accountable for their crimes. These cities protect criminals from being prosecuted and put on trial for the crimes they have committed. As a result, evil is protected and innocent lives are put at risk. By now you should understand this is a common thread within the Democrat Party. Whether it is abortion, gun control or secure borders… Democrats protect and enable criminals and the guilty and place innocent lives at risk.

XVII

KNEELING DURING THE
NATIONAL ANTHEM

Satan Appears as an Angle of Light:
Protesting or kneeling during the national anthem is free speech and
is a legal form of peaceful protest, which is a First Amendment right.

Satan's Goal: To malign a Christian country that stands for freedom
and equal rights. Create chaos, disorder and malign those keeping law
and order in society.

What does the Bible say? *"Bondservants, obey in all things your masters
according to the flesh, not with eyeservice, as men-pleasers, but in sincerity of heart,
fearing God. And whatever you do, do it heartily, as to the Lord and not to men,
knowing that from the Lord you will receive the reward of the inheritance; for you
serve the Lord Christ. But he who does wrong will be repaid for what he has done,
and there is no partiality."* (Colossians 3:22-25)

Kneeling during the national anthem began in the National
Football League (NFL), when a few players decided to protest what
they believed was the mistreatment of black Americans by the police.
As a result, while the national anthem was played before the start of
an NFL game, players would not stand, but instead kneel or raise
their fists (a symbol of black power). The players did this despite the
fact the NFL had a policy in place addressing standing during the
playing of the national anthem. Pages A62-63 of the league rulebook
states: "During the national anthem, players on the field and bench

area should stand at attention, face the flag, hold helmets in their left hand, and refrain from talking. The home team should ensure that the American flag is in good condition." "It should be pointed out to players and coaches that we continue to be judged by the public in this area of respect for the flag and our country. Failure to be on the field by the start of the national anthem result in discipline, such as fines, suspensions, and/or the forfeiture of draft choice(s) for violations of the above, including first offenses."

Von Miller, Denver Broncos linebacker said, "Me and my teammates, we felt like, we felt like President Trump's speech was an assault on our most cherished right -- freedom of speech."

Colin Kaepernick, former San Francisco 49ers quarterback said, "I am not going to stand up to show pride in a flag for a country that oppresses black people and people of color. To me, this is bigger than football and it would be selfish on my part to look the other way. There are bodies in the street and people getting paid leave and getting away with murder."

Panthers head coach Ron Rivera when asked about a player on his team kneeling during the national anthem said, "I'm not going to talk about a guy exercising his First Amendment rights."

NFL player Eric Reid said, "I feel I needed to regain control of that narrative and not let people say that what we're doing is un-American, because it's not. It's completely American. We're doing it because we want equality for everybody. We want our country to be a better place. So that's why I decided to resume the protest."

The NFL players that kneeled during the anthem were defying NFL rules. In time, the protest took on a life of its own and singers and cheerleaders began to follow the lead of these NFL players. Debate ensued and even President Trump weighed in on the players kneeling during the national anthem. President Trump chastised the players for disrespecting the flag and America. President Trump stated that action should be taken against kneeling NFL players such as a fine or suspension. However, some players continued to defy NFL policy and kneel during the national anthem. The NFL did not punish the players. The majority of American agreed with President Trump and NFL ratings and attendance declined.

Arguments in Support of Kneeling are Easily Disproven
There are two basic arguments in support of kneeling during the national anthem by players at sporting events. The first is that it is a form of free speech. The second is that it is a peaceful non-violent protest, against a wrong in society. Both arguments say that the protest is protected by the First Amendment right of free speech. Both arguments are incorrect and simple to disprove, with the same truth. That truth is that free speech and peaceful protests have limits and are not absolute.

Free Speech has Limits
Free speech and or peaceful protests are not allowed just anywhere and at any time. I do not know what they teach in school now, but I learned in fifth grade that you cannot yell fire in a crowded room, you cannot slander people and you cannot threaten people and call it free speech. All are crimes. If you believe free speech is absolute, go to a bank and say, "this is a stick up" or walk onto a plane and say, I have a bomb." If you do, you will be arrested.

If you believe those are extreme examples, try these: An angry employee for T-Mobile cannot yell and curse at a customer. A truck driver for Walmart cannot drive down the road and make obscene gestures out the window at traffic. Both are examples of free speech, but in both cases, the individual will be fired.

When a company is paying you to do a job, you must adhere to rules that company has in place. Some jobs require specific attire or uniforms. A cook is required to have netting or a hat. A waiter cannot work in their underwear. You want the salary of a bank manager? You just may have to wear a tie to work. A football player must wear a helmet and pads. A football player also cannot wear non-approved athletic equipment, cannot alter equipment or write on their uniforms. These are the rules. You may want to dress differently as part of your right of free speech, but you just may get fired.

Peaceful Protest Limits
There are limits to peaceful protests. A cashier at Walmart, cannot leave the register to join a protest outside when on the clock and say it is a First Amendment right. On the cashier's own time, but not on an employer's time, unless the employer allows you. When the cashier is at work, the cashier is under the authority of the employer. The

cashier must obey the policies of the employer. When you are at work, you are subject to your boss or supervisor and the rules of the company.

Order and Chain of Command

I talked about order in the chapter on sanctuary cities. There is always a protocol (chain of command) in ever organization and if it is not followed it leads to chaos. The NFL has a policy in place and it says that the players must stand and respect the national anthem or face fine, suspension or the team can lose a draft choice.

There is a chain of command in the NFL. At the top is the commissioner, next the owners and then the players. If the owners or an owner of a team says it is improper to kneel during the anthem, because it is against the policy of the NFL and they want to protect the team against penalties, the player or players must obey that authority.

However, the owners are subject to the commissioner. The commissioner has the final say. If the commissioner disagrees with the owner or owners, the owners must obey the commissioner. If not, then the owners can face penalties. Ultimately kneeling is not up to the players. The players cannot establish their own rules. It is up to the owners and then ultimately the commissioner.

The Houston Texans owner Bob McNair faced great backlash for saying NFL can't have 'inmates running the prison' regarding the national anthem protests. He is right. The players cannot be telling the owners and the commissioner what they want to do when it is against league rules. It would be the equivalent of a worker dictating policies to an owner or a CEO.

What Does the Bible Say About Kneeling During the Anthem

There was no national anthem when the Bible was written, however, the Bible says you are to respect authority... If your supervisor tells you to be at work at 8:00 am and you show up every day at 9:00 am, you will probably be fired. However, if the owner of the company, says it is okay to come in at 9:00 am, you can show up at 9:00 am. One thing is certain, you cannot show up anytime that you like. What does the Bible say?

The Bible says, *"Remind them to be subject to rulers and authorities, to obey, to be ready for every good work, to speak evil of no one, to be peaceable, gentle, showing all humility to all men."* (Titus 3:1-2)

You cannot have workers making the policies or not adhering to policies or there will be chaos. That is exactly what the NFL players are doing. It is no different than if workers decided to take 10 breaks a day and those in authority allowed it. It would create chaos and the company would suffer. What if employees of a company want to text all day on the job? Work that needed to be accomplished would not get done. I once worked with a girl that was on her phone all day texting. She was supposed to be watching individuals with extreme developmental disabilities. Individuals that needed assistance walking and or others that would have seizures. She was endangering the people she was paid to directly care for. She was told to put her phone away and stop texting numerous times. She would not. As a result, she was fired.

The Bible says, *"Bondservants, obey in all things your masters according to the flesh, not with eyeservice, as men-pleasers, but in sincerity of heart, fearing God. And whatever you do, do it heartily, as to the Lord and not to men, knowing that from the Lord you will receive the reward of the inheritance; for you serve the Lord Christ. But he who does wrong will be repaid for what he has done, and there is no partiality."* (Colossians 3:22-25)

The Bible says that you are to do what your superiors tell you to do and not just the minimum. You are to do your best. In everything that you do, work from the heart for God, because it is God who you really serve. These NFL players are rebelling against authority.

Democrats and Rebellion

I would like to address one last issue here, because Satan always perverts what is meant for good. Democrats and liberals always say that their protests arise to stop some injustice. However, with this book, I am pointing out that their entire platform is not Biblical. As a result, when they protest, they are protesting what is right in the eyes of God. There is only one reason to stand up against authority and it is when that authority is doing things that are not Godly. If a supervisor is requiring you to embezzle money, that is stealing. If a supervisor is requiring you to falsify records, that is lying. In these instances, you would not obey authority.

When Peter and the Apostles were teaching at the temple, they were arrested and told not to preach about Jesus. When they were found to be continuing to preach about Jesus, they were brought before the council for disobeying authority.

The Bible says, *"But Peter and the other apostles answered and said: "We ought to obey God rather than men."* (Acts 5:29).

When the laws established by people conflict with the laws of God, you are to obey God. In the book of Daniel, King Nebuchadnezzar made an edict that everyone was to worship a gold statute. Shadrach, Meshach and Abednego did not comply. They would not worship the statue, but worshipped God instead. King Nebuchadnezzar threw them into a furnace to burn to death. However, they did not die, God protected them. What if a president signed an executive order that said everyone must worship the tallest building in America? Are you to obey that order and worship a building? No, because the Bible says that is idolatry and you are to worship God!

In the sixth chapter of the book of Daniel, Darius the king established a law that for thirty days no one could pray other than Darius himself. Daniel got on his knees and prayed to God despite the law. He was then thrown into a lion's den to be killed. God shut the mouths of the lions protecting Daniel and he did not die. Again, we are to obey God when laws created by people are contrary to the word of God.

Democrats and liberals say they are protesting (rebelling) against what they believe is right. Take note that it is what they believe in their own eyes and not what the Bible says. These individuals lack the knowledge of God and are twisting the truth. They are rebelling against the word of God. They protest in support of gay marriage, abortion, open borders, legalization of drugs…. They are rebelling with Satan and his demons against God. They are obeying the laws of man rather than the word of God.

XVIII

TESTS, TRIALS AND PERSECUTION

Satan Appears as an Angel of Light: There is no need for anyone to struggle or suffer in life. Society needs to be fair for everyone and no one should be disadvantaged.

Satan's Goal: Stifle growth and success to make you weak.

What does the Bible say?
Tests: *"But as we have been approved by God to be entrusted with the gospel, even so we speak, not as pleasing men, but God who tests our hearts."* (1 Thessalonians 2:4)

Trials: *"My brethren, count it all joy when you fall into various trials, knowing that the testing of your faith produces patience. But let patience have its perfect work, that you may be perfect and complete, lacking nothing."* (James 1:2-4)

Persecution: *"Remember the word that I said to you, 'A servant is not greater than his master.' If they persecuted Me, they will also persecute you. If they kept My word, they will keep yours also. But all these things they will do to you for My name's sake, because they do not know Him who sent Me."* (John 15:20-21)

The topic of tests, trials and persecution is an entire book to itself. However, I want to touch on each to explain the difference between them and show that it is not possible to eliminate them from life. It is the Democrat Party that desires a level playing field to make life the same for all and to reduce the struggles in life, which is just not possible.

To understand, I once got into a discussion regarding abortion with a very liberal Democrat. She stated to me, "it is better for a child to be aborted than a single mother struggle in life working hard to support a child while trying to get an education." I thought to myself, "if that is the standard, why not allow murder if someone gets in your way?" Does she believe people with disabilities should be put to death, because they are going to struggle in life?

Every person has God given abilities and talents. Every person's path in life, their successes and struggles are going to be different. A struggle for one person may not be a struggle to another. I think fighting traffic to get to work and back home is a great struggle. I have a friend that does not mind traffic and listens to self-improvement teachings when driving. Some people think struggling is working the night before a big exam. Personally, I loved the pressure and challenge of studying for exams with a limited time frame. The pressure forced me to concentrate on the subject matter. Struggles vary from person to person, so what struggles are we to eliminate? It is just not possible to eliminate struggles. This is especially true, if you want to accomplish something worthwhile. Open your own business and you will go through some great struggles complying with business regulations, taxes, inventories, employees and customers…

What this liberal Democrat also does not understand is the difference between, tests, trials and persecution.

Tests

What are tests? Tests are activities (such as a series of questions or exercises) for measuring the skill, knowledge, capacities or aptitudes of an individual or a group. Test are good for you! A good father tests his children. He gives them chores and responsibilities to measure their maturity and help them grow. A good father evaluates the results to see where the child needs to improve. A good teacher tests their students. A good teacher wants to see where a student stands in relation to their progress of learning a subject. A good teacher wants the student to be knowledgeable so when they move on whether it is higher education or in the workforce, they succeed.

Tests are needed in life to grow and to assess where you are in relation to progress of a goal… Tests tell you areas where you are competent and areas where you need to improve. Tests are a necessary part of life.

In the workforce, there are tests every day to see if you can handle further responsibility. These tests include showing up at work on time, completing tasks when they are due, getting your workload finished, treating customers well and resolving customer issues. You are always being tested and if you pass the tests you progress, improve and then may get promoted. If you cannot show up to work on time, finish tasks timely or treat customers well, there would be no reason for promotion. It would be counterproductive for any organization to promote a person with such behavior.

A medical doctor must first obtain a bachelor's degree and then successfully complete medical school. Once those tests are passed, there are more. A residency at a hospital must be completed and the licensing must be completed. These are all tests… Imagine a world without tests? If you went to a hospital, how would you know if the doctor was qualified? How would you like to have surgery, if the surgeon never had to pass any tests to work in a hospital? What if this was the standard in society? There would be failure, disaster and chaos everywhere. Again, this is what Satan and the Democrat Party desire.

God Gives Tests

Tests are good and necessary in life. Tests are so important that the Bible says that God tests you as well. God gives people tests in life and in ministry. In ministry, God tests your heart to see if He can trust you to preach the Gospel faithfully.

The Bible says, *"But as we have been approved by God to be entrusted with the gospel, even so we speak, not as pleasing men, but God who tests our hearts."* (1 Thessalonians 2:4)

You will start in ministry (serving) by doing very basic duties in the church. It may as a greeter, an usher or even setting up banquets... God tests you to see if you are you faithful. He wants to see if you cause division, if you complain, if you show love to people and if you represent the church accordingly? Joyce Meyer said, "Sometimes God allows us to be tested because He's preparing us for promotion." As you pass His tests and grow, God gives you more responsibility. With time, you may be teaching a Bible study or helping the pastor. If God sees that you are faithful, and you pass His tests, you may have your own church. If you fail the tests that you are given, you learn where you need to improve. If you do not change or improve, you may not be serving the church at all.

The Bible says, *"I, the Lord, search the heart, I test the mind, Even to give every man according to his ways, According to the fruit of his doings."* (Jeremiah 17:10)

When I first started serving in the church, I passed out communion during service. I then served in other capacities, such as helping with new member banquets, providing security during construction of a new church at night, setting up chairs at events, introducing speakers at prayer events... It took years of serving and learning and passing tests. Eventually, God trusted me enough to plant my own church. God sees how we handle the tests that He gives us and rewards us accordingly. The Bible says that God does not only test us, but He watches us:

"The Lord is in His holy temple, The Lord's throne is in heaven; His eyes behold, His eyelids test the sons of men. The Lord tests the righteous, But the wicked and the one who loves violence His soul hates." (Psalm 11:4-5)

Jesus Tested the Disciples

Jesus tested the disciples. If He tested them, be sure that He will test you! When Jesus performed the miracle of feeding the five thousand, He tested the faith of Phillip. Jesus had finished preaching and there were thousands of people that were hungry, but there were only five barley loaves and two fish.

The Bible says, *"Now the Passover, a feast of the Jews, was near. Then Jesus lifted up His eyes, and seeing a great multitude coming toward Him, He said to Philip, "Where shall we buy bread, that these may eat?" But this He said to test him, for He Himself knew what He would do."* (John 6:5-6)

Jesus knew He was going to perform a miracle and feed the multitude of people with the little food that was present. However, Jesus asked Phillip where they could buy bread? The Bible says it was a test, because Jesus already knew what He was going to do. I am certain that Phillip learned a great lesson about never doubting Jesus again.

The point is that we all face tests in life, there is no way to eliminate them. The tests between becoming a beautician, school teacher and a doctor will be different. You should be grateful for your tests and embrace them. Tests keep order in society, they help you learn, grow and become better…

The Bible says, *"For You, O God, have tested us; You have refined us as silver is refined."* (Psalm 66:10)

Trials

Trials are different than tests. A definition of trial is patience, or stamina through subjection to suffering or temptation. When I think of trials. I think of a person that goes on trial in court. The person broke a law, did something wrong and now is on trial. Trials are difficult. Trials are hardships.

God does not give us trials. Trials are from Satan. They are the result of our own disobedience to God. They are the result of our sin. God allows them to happen, because of the law of sowing and reaping. God allows trials to teach you. It would not be proper for someone to do wrong and face no trial or hardship, because without consequence, there would be no change of behavior. However, this is what the Democrat Party desires. They want no personal responsibility for poor behavior or sin. If you do not want to work, there will be no consequences, they will take care of you.

Let me give you an example to explain the difference between tests and trials. In school, you have exams (tests) to take. If you do not study and fail the tests, that failure would result in trials. You may have to go to summer school or be left back a year. At your job, you will have responsibilities (tests) to complete. Showing up to work on time is a test. If you do not pass the tests, you can lose your job. If you are unemployed, you will then face financial struggles (trials).

A father will test a child by giving chores (tests) to complete. If the child completes the chores, the tests are passed. As a result, there are rewards such as compensation (an allowance) and promotion (greater chores). In time, the child also learns responsibility, discipline, how to follow instructions, order, skills and how to use tools. The child also earns money and learns to spend and save. In time, accumulating enough money to purchase things such as a car. The child also earns the favor of the father.

However, if the child does not do chores as told, is not responsible and fails the tests, there may be some consequences. The child will not be given greater responsibility, learn skills, given more responsibility and will earn less money. The child will also not build good habits of discipline, learn how to fix things and use tools. The child may not accumulate money to buy things such as a car. The child will then have a hardship (trial) of getting to places with no transportation. The trial was the result of poor behavior. A good father will allow that hardship (trial) in order that the child learn to be responsible and do chores correctly. If father purchased a car for the child regardless of the failed tests, what did the child learn? The child learned not to be responsible and still get rewarded. The child will also have not earned favor with the father. The same is true with God. God will not bless you for sinful behavior and you will not earn His favor.

Again, God forgives you of sin when you repent. However, he does not absolve you of the consequences of your sin. The reason is so you to learn from your sin and to turn from sinful behavior. If you steal, God will forgive you, but you may end up in jail.

The ultimate example of trials is the book of Job. God allowed Satan to place hardship (trials) on Job. God did not put Job through these trials, God allowed Satan to put Job through trials. It was because of Job's sin, which was self-righteousness. The Bible says, Job justified himself rather than God. For almost the entire book, Job said compare me to anyone, I am righteous and innocent. We are righteous because of God not because of what we do.

The Bible says, *"So these three men ceased answering Job, because he was righteous in his own eyes. Then the wrath of Elihu, the son of Barachel the Buzite, of the family of Ram, was aroused against Job; his wrath was aroused because he justified himself rather than God."* (Job 32:1-2)

Job lost everything except for his own life and his wife. He lost his oxen, donkeys, his sheep and camels. These animals allowed Job to work the field which provided food and they also provided transportation. Job also lost his children and his health...

Eventually, God questions Job directly. It is done to teach Job a lesson about being self-righteous. Anyone who is oppressed with pride (thinks they are so much better than everyone else) should listen to the questioning of Job by God. It will put into perspective how small you are in comparison to God. If you have any pride in you, I ask that you read this scripture as if God is talking to you directly, because He is.

The Bible says that God questioned Job, *"Where were you when I laid the foundations of the earth? Tell Me, if you have understanding. Who determined its measurements? Surely you know! Or who stretched the line upon it? To what were its foundations fastened? Or who laid its cornerstone, When the morning stars sang together, And all the sons of God shouted for joy? "Or who shut in the sea with doors, When it burst forth and issued from the womb; When I made the clouds its garment, And thick darkness its swaddling band; When I fixed My limit for it, And set bars and doors; When I said, 'This far you may come, but no farther, And here your proud waves must stop!' "Have you commanded the morning since your days began, And caused the dawn to know its place, That it might take hold of the ends of the earth, And the wicked be shaken out of it? It takes on form like clay under a seal, And stands out like a garment. From the wicked their light is withheld, And the upraised arm is broken. "Have you entered the springs of the sea? Or have you walked in search of the depths? Have the gates of death been revealed to you? Or have you seen the doors of the shadow of death? Have you comprehended the breadth of the earth? Tell Me, if you know all this. "Where is the way to the dwelling of light? And darkness, where is its place, That you may take it to its territory, That you may know the paths to its home? Do you know it, because you were born then, Or because the number of your days is great? "Have you entered the treasury of snow, Or have you seen the treasury of hail, Which I have reserved for the time of trouble, For the day of battle and war? By what way is light diffused, Or the east wind scattered over the earth? "Who has divided a channel for the overflowing water, Or a path for the thunderbolt, To cause it to rain on a land where there is no one, A wilderness in which there is no man; To satisfy the desolate waste, And cause to spring forth the growth of tender grass? Has the rain a father? Or who has begotten the drops of dew? From whose womb comes the ice? And the frost of heaven, who gives it birth? The waters harden like stone, And the surface of the deep is frozen. "Can you bind the cluster of the Pleiades, Or loose the belt of Orion? Can you bring out Mazzaroth in its season? Or can you guide the Great Bear with its cubs? Do you know the ordinances of the heavens? Can you set their dominion over the earth?*

"Can you lift up your voice to the clouds, That an abundance of water may cover you? Can you send out lightnings, that they may go, And say to you, 'Here we are!'? Who has put wisdom in the mind? Or who has given understanding to the heart? Who can number the clouds by wisdom? Or who can pour out the bottles of heaven, When the dust hardens in clumps, And the clods cling together?
"Can you hunt the prey for the lion, Or satisfy the appetite of the young lions, When they crouch in their dens, Or lurk in their lairs to lie in wait? Who provides food for the raven, When its young ones cry to God, And wander about for lack of food?" (Job 38:4-41)

Have you been delivered from your pride? I hope and pray that you have so you do not have to go through trials for God to teach you to be humble. God continues to question Job through all of chapter 39. I challenge you to read it.

In chapter 40, the Bible says, *"Moreover the Lord answered Job, and said: "Shall the one who contends with the Almighty correct Him? He who rebukes God, let him answer it."*

God asks Job, do you want to challenge Me? Do you want to argue with Me? If so, correct Me and tell Me the answers to the question I asked.

The Bible says, *"Then Job answered the Lord: "I am not worthy to speak! What can I say to you? I cannot answer you! I will put my hand over my mouth. I spoke once, but I will not speak again. I spoke twice, but I will not say anything more."* (Job 40: 3-5)

Job cannot answer God. It is not possible to have the wisdom and knowledge of God. Job says he will put his hand over his mouth and not speak. You would think that would be the end, however, God continues to question Job.

The Bible says, *"Then the Lord answered Job out of the whirlwind, and said: "Now prepare yourself like a man; I will question you, and you shall answer Me: "Would you indeed annul My judgment? Would you condemn Me that you may be justified? Have you an arm like God? Or can you thunder with a voice like His? Then adorn yourself with majesty and splendor, And array yourself with glory and beauty."* (Job 40:6-10)

God continues to question Job through the rest of chapters 40 and 41. I challenge you to read it also. Finally, Job answers God after all the questions…

The Bible says, *"Then Job answered the Lord and said: "I know that You can do everything, And that no purpose of Yours can be withheld from You. You asked, 'Who is this who hides counsel without knowledge?' Therefore I have uttered what I did not understand, Things too wonderful for me, which I did not know. Listen, please, and let me speak; You said, 'I will question you, and you shall answer Me.' "I have heard of You by the hearing of the ear, But now my eye sees You. Therefore I abhor myself,*
And repent in dust and ashes." (Job 42:1-6)

Job admits that he does not understand what he was saying. Job repents for his sin of self-righteousness. A once self-righteous Job learned a lesson about pride. God allowed Job to go through the worst possible trials imaginable because of his sin. The trials were not from God, they were from Satan. The trials were allowed by God. Sin will cause us to go through trials in life. God allows those trials to teach us valuable lessons about sin. Through the trials, Job never spoke against God and remained faithful. In the end, Job learned about pride and that he was not so self-righteousness. It was only until Job realized the truth and repented that God then restored all that Job had.

The Bible says, *"Now the Lord blessed the latter days of Job more than his beginning;"* (Job 42:12)

All Things Work Together for Good to Those who Love God
This is what you need to understand, each one of us sin and we do not have the knowledge and wisdom of God. As a result, we will all go through trials. It is through those trials that we can learn and should repent. If you do not learn and repent, you will continue to go through more trials until you do.

Chuck Colson was part of the Nixon Administration in the 1970's. In 1974, he was indicted for conspiring to cover up the Watergate burglaries. Colson pleaded guilty to obstruction of justice. Colson faced a trial, because of things that he did in life. It was due to his own actions. Colson was subsequently sentenced to prison. Before entering prison, Colson gave his life to the Lord. During his time in prison, Colson ministered to other inmates. When he completed his sentence, Colson said he would devote the rest of his life to Christian ministry. In 1976, he founded Prison Fellowship Ministries, an organization that would preach the Gospel in prisons around the world. It became the world's largest prison ministry. Colson saw the truth, repented, loved God and was restored.

Many people do not respond to their trials in such a Godly or positive manner. I gave the example of the young man in Pine Hills who was not living for God. He had dropped out of school, was stealing, using drugs, dealing drugs and sentenced to prison… His trials were great. He told us that he had wished he had listened to us, when he first met him. It is not too late for him to turn his life around, however, in the meantime is trials will get worse if he does not learn, repent and love God.

No matter what sins you have committed or trials you go through in life, God can restore you. You must learn the truth, repent and love God. God will then use those circumstances and trials for good. Drug addicts have been delivered from addition, thieves delivered from stealing and murderers delivered from murdering. Once someone has found God and repented, God will use them to minister to others.

The Bible says, *"And we know that all things work together for good to those who love God, to those who are the called according to His purpose."* (Romans 8:28)

Joel Osteen said, "The Bible talks about how God uses difficult situations to develop our character and get us stronger."

Warren Wiersbe said, "Let the trials of life make you a giant, not a midget."

Charles Spurgeon "Many men owe the grandeur of their lives to their tremendous difficulties."

The Bible says, *"My brethren, count it all joy when you fall into various trials, knowing that the testing of your faith produces patience. But let patience have its perfect work, that you may be perfect and complete, lacking nothing."* (James 1:2-8)

Persecution

Persecution is not a test and it is not a trial. Persecution is an attack against you solely based on the fact you are a Christian. A definition of persecution is hostility and ill-treatment, because of religious beliefs. Persecution is from Satan. Those doing the persecution are listening to Satan and his demons and not God. Those persecuting Christians are demon possessed or oppressed and want to stay in their sin.

It is the Democrat Party and their supporters that protest the things of God. They ridicule Christians, call them names and arrest them for defending the Bible. You will be hated and then you will be persecuted… and it is in that order. Democrat Party is a platform for persecution of Christians.

Democrat President Barak Obama used the power of the federal government to persecute the Tea Party, Republicans and Christians. In American government, there is the separation of powers. There are equal branches of government, which are federal, judicial and legislative. The equal branches of government were created so that there would not be an abuse of power. However, when a government official uses the powers of government to attack their enemies, it is called soft tyranny. It is a soft form of dictatorship and an abuse of power. Obama had those that spoke out against him audited by the IRS and he had businesses owned by Republicans and Christians targeted by federal agencies like the EPA.

In 2011, federal agents raided Gibson Guitar Corp. facilities in Nashville and Memphis, Tenn., and seized several pallets of wood, electronic files and guitars. Gibson was accused of using wood illegally obtained to make their guitars. Gibson's chief executive, Henry Juszkiewicz, was a supporter of the Republican Party.

The Billy Graham Evangelistic Association came out and said, Obama's IRS Was "targeting and attempting to intimidate us." Franklin Graham, the president of the Billy Graham Evangelistic

Association said, "while these audits not only wasted taxpayer money, they wasted money contributed by donors for ministry purposes as we had to spend precious resources servicing the IRS agents in our offices."

Democrats have censored sermons from pastors, fired public officials because of mentioning scripture, punished bakers, florists, and wedding photographers with massive fines simply for wanting to practice their Christian faith. A Kentucky clerk of the court was jailed for refusing to issue a marriage license to gay couples. A Canadian man faced two years in prison for passing out "Jesus Saves" pamphlets at a gay pride parade.

The Deep State

Most recently, something labeled the "Deep State" is an example of persecution by the Democrat Party. Employees of the Justice Department and FBI hired by Democrat President Barrack Obama targeted Republican Donald Trump by falsifying information to stop and then attempt to bring down his presidency. A special counsel was appointed to investigate the falsified evidence. The special counsel then targeted Trump and his associates, investigating all aspects of their lives… However, the special counsel did not target any Democrats…

Democrats and Muslims

People ask the question, why do Democrats attack and persecute Christians, but not Muslims? The answer is that they have the same goal in common. That goal is to eliminate Jesus from society. I will say this, if Mohammed really was a God, the Democrats would attack the Muslim religion and they do not. It is proof the Muslim religion is demonic.

What the Bible says about Persecution

The Bible says, *"Remember the word that I said to you, 'A servant is not greater than his master.' If they persecuted Me, they will also persecute you. If they kept My word, they will keep yours also. But all these things they will do to you for My name's sake, because they do not know Him who sent Me."* (John 15:20-21)

Special Favor from God

The Bible tells us that there is hope. Jesus knew you would be persecuted. Do you think Jesus would not offer you rewards for believing in Him and enduring such persecution? The Bible says that if you are persecuted for your faith, you will be blessed and that means that you have special favor from God.

"Blessed are you when men hate you, And when they exclude you, And revile you, and cast out your name as evil, For the Son of Man's sake. (Luke 6:22)

"Blessed are those who are persecuted for righteousness' sake, For theirs is the kingdom of heaven." (Matthew 5:10-12)

"But even if you should suffer for righteousness' sake, you are blessed. "And do not be afraid of their threats, nor be troubled." (1 Peter 3:14-16)

"Blessed are you when they revile and persecute you, and say all kinds of evil against you falsely for My sake. Rejoice and be exceedingly glad, for great is your reward in heaven, for so they persecuted the prophets who were before you." (Matthew 5:11-12)

When you are persecuted for your Christian faith, know the Kingdom of God is inside of you. Look at it as a badge of honor, knowing that you stand with God against evil. Also know that you are going to be blessed.

The Bible says that God is your friend. I ask people the question, "wouldn't it be nice to be friends with Bill Gates or Donald Trump or a rich celebrity and have them in your speed dial?" People usually say, "yes". Then I ask them, "if you did something wrong and hurt their feelings, wouldn't you apologize and ask for forgiveness?" People say, "yes". However, what could these individuals do for you? They could build you a house or give you some money, but it is all temporary…

I ask you who are reading this to stamp your foot on the ground. God created the earth under your feet. Next look up at the sky or the stars at night. God created the entire universe, further than the eye can see. He can do more for you than any person on this earth. There is no speed dialing required. If you have done something that has offended God, repent and ask forgiveness. God is your greatest

friend. And if you are being persecuted, do not be discouraged. God
will be faithful and He will bless you!

BONUS CHAPTERS

XIX

THE MESSIANIC PROPHECIES

One of the first sermons that I ever preached was about the Messianic Prophecies in the Old Testament about a coming Messiah. When I first learned of them, it left no doubt for me that Jesus was God. I could cite numerous theological arguments, but overwhelmingly it is that Jesus fulfilled all the prophecies documented in the Old Testament of a coming Messiah. Jesus is the only person to walk the earth to do so.

The Bible was written by 40 authors over a period of 1,500 years, on different continents and different languages. There are no contradictions and it is in perfect harmony, from beginning to end. The human mind can hardly comprehend fulfilling every Messianic prophecy in the Old Testament because many are still being uncovered today. Let me explain it this way. The chances of winning the lottery in the United States are very small, 50 million to 1. Currently, there are 7 billion people on earth. If there was a world lottery, the chances would be even less. Add to that all the people that had ever lived and have passed on and it would be billions of more people. There is only one person who ever walked the earth that fulfilled every one of the prophecies in the Old Testament about a coming Messiah and it was Jesus…

To understand the messianic prophecies, you must first understand that God spoke through prophets to tell the world about a coming messiah. God wanted the world to recognize Him, because there would many who would claim to be Him. From 1500 years to hundreds of years before the birth of Jesus, these prophets gave a detailed description of when the messiah would come, what he would do and what He would experience.

The Bible says, *"I have also spoken by the prophets, And have multiplied visions; I have given symbols through the witness of the prophets."* (Hosea 12:10)

These prophets were inspired not by their own wisdom and thought, but by the Holy Spirit.

The Bible says, *"that no prophecy of Scripture is of any private interpretation, for prophecy never came by the will of man, but holy men of God spoke as they were moved by the Holy Spirit."* (2 Peter 1:20-21)

To list all the prophecies would be a book to itself. They can easily be found on the internet. However, I will provide a short summary of some of these prophecies. The Old Testament said the messiah would be born of a virgin, would be born in Bethlehem, would come according to a timetable, would be the seed of a woman, the descendant of Abraham through whom all nations would be blessed, would be called a Nazarene, would bring in a new covenant, would be preceded by a messenger, would perform signs of healing, would be a suffering servant, would be called out of Egypt, would be a prophet like Moses, would come riding on a donkey, would be greater than David, would be betrayed for thirty pieces of silver, would be the object of a murderous plot, would be scourged, would be a willing sacrifice, would be the Passover lamb, would be pierced, would be forsaken, would be the rejected cornerstone and would be resurrected. These are just a few of the hundreds of messianic prophecies in the Old Testament and Jesus fulfilled every single one. In fact, Jesus is in every book of the Bible.
Rick Warren said, "the New Testament is hidden in the Old

Testament and the Old Testament is revealed in the New Testament." It is not just these prophecies that Jesus fulfills, but there are entire passages of scripture in the Old Testament that are prophecies that Jesus fulfilled. I am going to cite a scripture below from the book of Leviticus to demonstrate how the Bible is written in symbolic language, how Jesus is in every book of the Bible and how the New Testament is hidden in the Old Testament.

The Ritual for Cleansing Healed Lepers

"Then the Lord spoke to Moses, saying, "This shall be the law of the leper for the day of his cleansing: He shall be brought to the priest. And the priest shall go out of the camp, and the priest shall examine him; and indeed, if the leprosy is healed in the leper, then the priest shall command to take for him who is to be cleansed two living and clean birds, cedar wood, scarlet, and hyssop. And the priest shall command that one of the birds be killed in an earthen vessel over running water. As for the living bird, he shall take it, the cedar wood and the scarlet and the hyssop, and dip them and the living bird in the blood of the bird that was killed over the running water. And he shall sprinkle it seven times on him who is to be cleansed from the leprosy, and shall pronounce him clean, and shall let the living bird loose in the open field." (Leviticus 14:1-7)

When you read this scripture of the cleansing of the leper by the priest, I am certain you are thinking, "what does this mean?" When I was first read this scripture, it meant nothing to me. In fact, it was quite confusing and a bit boring. Without the context and the knowledge of Jesus, it does not make a lot of sense. But when you understand how the Bible is written, it is captivating! The cleansing of the leper by the priest is a Messianic Prophecy written 1400 years before Jesus was born.

In the Old Testament, the priest represents Jesus and leprosy represents sin. We are to go to Jesus to cleanse our sins like the lepers were to go to the priest. Cedar is symbolic of the cross, hyssop represents faith and scarlet the suffering savior. One bird killed in an earthen vessel, is symbolic of Jesus killed in His earthen vessel (His body). The leper sprinkled seven times with blood, represents that the blood of Jesus was shed seven times while He was on earth. The blood from the bird was sprinkled using the hyssop, representing that faith is essential in the process of cleansing from sin. The second bird let loose is symbolic of the resurrection of Jesus. The leper pronounced cleansed by the priest, represents our sins being cleansed by the blood of Jesus. This is the foreshadowing of Jesus, written 1500 years before His birth. It is one of the hundreds of messianic prophecies that Jesus fulfilled.

XX

THE CHRISTMAS STORY

The Bible says, *"For God so loved the world that He gave His only begotten Son, that whoever believes in Him should not perish but have everlasting life."* (John 3:16)

The Bible says that Jesus was a gift to us from God. The definition of gift is something given willingly to someone without payment. There is no gift that you will ever get that can compare to the gift of Jesus. All other gifts are temporary and finite. This gift, if you accept it, brings eternal life in heaven.

Once you accept the gift of Jesus, the next step is what to do with the gift? Like all gifts, you can set it aside or use it in your life. Some gifts are simple, others are more complex and need instruction manuals. Jesus was God, so I think He would require some instructions. The Bible says Jesus was such a precious gift that Paul called this gift indescribable. The Bible says, *"Thanks be to God for His indescribable gift!"* (2 Corinthians 9:15). To truly understand the precious indescribable gift of Jesus, you need an instruction manual. Fortunately, God gave you one.

The Christmas Story paints a picture of something more than the events surrounding the birth of Jesus. It is an instruction manual for how you are to treat this indescribable gift.

Christ's Birth Announced to Mary

The Bible says, *"Now in the sixth month the angel Gabriel was sent by God to a city of Galilee named Nazareth, to a virgin betrothed to a man whose name was Joseph, of the house of David. The virgin's name was Mary. And having come in, the angel said to her, "Rejoice, highly favored one, the Lord is with you; blessed are you among women!" But when she saw him, she was troubled at his saying, and considered what manner of greeting this was. Then the angel said to her, "Do not be afraid, Mary, for you have found favor with God. And behold, you will conceive in your womb and bring forth a Son, and shall call His name Jesus. He will be great, and will be called the Son of the Highest; and the Lord God will give Him the throne of His father David. And He will reign over the house of Jacob forever, and of His kingdom there will be no end." Then Mary said to the angel, "How can this be, since I do not know a man?" And the angel answered and said to her, "The Holy Spirit will come upon you, and the power of the Highest will overshadow you; therefore, also, that Holy One who is to be born will be called the Son of God. Now indeed, Elizabeth your relative has also conceived a son in her old age; and this is now the sixth month for her who was called barren. For with God nothing will be impossible." Then Mary said, "Behold the maidservant of the Lord! Let it be to me according to your word." And the angel departed from her."* (Luke 1:26-38)

God is going to speak to you to do His work on this earth, which is delivering Jesus to the world. Do not be afraid! Mary was given the task of delivering Jesus to the world and faced the consequences of ridicule, scorn, losing her fiancé and even death by stoning. That was the punishment at that time for becoming pregnant before marriage. In the scripture above it says, *the power of the Highest will overshadow you.* Overshadow means to protect. God protected Mary for doing His will. You must be obedient and do the will of God. You may face those same obstacles as Mary delivering Jesus to the world, but God will perform miracles and He will protect you.

As I noted, my wife and I planted a church in Pine Hills, Florida. It was one of the most crime filled cities in all of Florida. In our first year, within a 10-mile radius of our church there were a dozen murders. We heard gunshots at night on a regular basis. There were helicopters overhead each day searching for people that were evading the law. However, we would do all night prayer meetings and walk the streets at 5 am praying. My wife would drive through the streets during the day, stop and randomly pray for people. Grown men were breaking down like babies and crying when they got prayed for… God always protected us. We were never afraid. If you do the Lord's work delivering Jesus to the world, God will protect you.

Christ Born of Mary

The Bible says, *"Now the birth of Jesus Christ was as follows: After His mother Mary was betrothed to Joseph, before they came together, she was found with child of the Holy Spirit. Then Joseph her husband, being a just man, and not wanting to make her a public example, was minded to put her away secretly. But while he thought about these things, behold, an angel of the Lord appeared to him in a dream, saying, "Joseph, son of David, do not be afraid to take to you Mary your wife, for that which is conceived in her is of the Holy Spirit. And she will bring forth a Son, and you shall call His name Jesus, for He will save His people from their sins." So all this was done that it might be fulfilled which was spoken by the Lord through the prophet, saying: 23 "Behold, the virgin shall be with child, and bear a Son, and they shall call His name Immanuel," which is translated, "God with us." Then Joseph, being aroused from sleep, did as the angel of the Lord commanded him and took to him his wife, and did not know her till she had brought forth her firstborn Son. And he called His name Jesus.* (Matthew 1:18-25)

God will speak to you, in your dreams. You must listen to God and you will know it is Him when it aligns with His word. Joseph protected Mary and helped her deliver Jesus to the world. Joseph could have lived a selfish life and walked away from Mary, but he did not. When you know someone that is delivering Jesus to the world, you must protect them. God expects you to. You must be obedient like Joseph. Anyone that is preaching the Gospel in the many ways that it is possible, protect those people and help them deliver Jesus to the world.

Mary and Joseph Comply with the Census

The Bible says, *"And it came to pass in those days that a decree went out from Caesar Augustus that all the world should be registered. ²This census first took place while Quirinius was governing Syria. So all went to be registered, everyone to his own city. Joseph also went up from Galilee, out of the city of Nazareth, into Judea, to the city of David, which is called Bethlehem, because he was of the house and lineage of David, to be registered with Mary, his betrothed wife, who was with child. So it was, that while they were there, the days were completed for her to be delivered."* (Luke 2:1-6)

When Mary was about to give birth to Jesus (deliver Him to the world), Joseph was required to comply with a government census. To do so, he and Mary (while nine months pregnant) would have to travel more than 90 miles by donkey from Nazareth to Bethlehem. They did not let the requirements and obligations of society stop them. While you are called to deliver Jesus to the world, you will have to comply with government regulations. You have responsibilities as citizens in society. You will have to pay property taxes, file income taxes, register your car, mow your yard… You cannot forsake your responsibilities to society because you want to deliver Jesus to the world. It may be arduous, it may be difficult or inconvenient, but you must be a good citizen.

Mary Delivers Jesus

The Bible says, *"And she brought forth her firstborn Son, and wrapped Him in swaddling cloths, and laid Him in a manger, because there was no room for them in the inn."* (Luke 2:7)

Mary delivered Jesus to the world in the feeding trough of a stable. Where else would the lamb of God be born, except in a stable? You are going to have to go to some places that you do not want to go to deliver Jesus to the world. It may be in a poverty-stricken inner city or a third world country. You must go, wherever God calls you. Everyone needs to hear the Gospel. The Bible says, *"Go into all the world and preach the gospel."* It does not say to go to only wealthy areas or areas that you feel comfortable. I once heard of a pastor who would travel through the back woods of India and baptize people in dirty rivers. My wife and I moved to a dangerous crime filled and impoverished city, where we were the minority, to preach the Gospel. We changed many lives there… It turned out to be the greatest experience of my life.

Wise Men from the East

The Bible says, *"Then Herod, when he had secretly called the wise men, determined from them what time the star appeared. And he sent them to Bethlehem and said, "Go and search carefully for the young Child, and when you have found Him, bring back word to me, that I may come and worship Him also." When they heard the king, they departed; and behold, the star which they had seen in the East went before them, till it came and stood over where the young Child was. When they saw the star, they rejoiced with exceedingly great joy. And when they had come into the house, they saw the young Child with Mary His mother, and fell down and worshiped Him. And when they had opened their treasures, they presented gifts to Him: gold, frankincense, and myrrh. Then, being divinely warned in a dream that they should not return to Herod, they departed for their own country another way."* (Matthew 2:7-12)

King Herod tried to trick the wise men by saying that he wanted to worship the Child (Jesus). Herod really wanted to find Jesus to kill Him. The world wants to eliminate Jesus from society and they will go to great lengths to do so. The world turns Christmas into Santa Claus and happy holidays. The world turns Easter into a bunny…. Once again, God spoke in a dream and the wisemen listened. The wise men did not listen to Herod. They worshipped Jesus and then they gave Him their best. You are to not listen to the world that wants to eliminate Jesus. You are to worship Jesus and you are to give Him your best.

Glory to God in the Highest

The Bible says, *"Now there were in the same country shepherds living out in the fields, keeping watch over their flock by night. And behold, an angel of the Lord stood before them, and the glory of the Lord shone around them, and they were greatly afraid. Then the angel said to them, "Do not be afraid, for behold, I bring you good tidings of great joy which will be to all people. For there is born to you this day in the city of David a Savior, who is Christ the Lord. And this will be the sign to you: You will find a Babe wrapped in swaddling cloths, lying in a manger." And suddenly there was with the angel a multitude of the heavenly host praising God and saying: "Glory to God in the highest And on earth peace, goodwill toward men!" So it was, when the angels had gone away from them into heaven, that the shepherds said to one another, "Let us now go to Bethlehem and see this thing that has come to pass, which the Lord has made known to us." And they came with haste and found Mary and Joseph, and the Babe lying in a manger. Now when they had seen Him, they made widely known the saying which was told them concerning this Child. And all those who heard it marveled at those things which were told them by the shepherds. But Mary kept all these things and pondered them in her heart. Then the shepherds returned, glorifying and praising God for all the things that they had heard and seen, as it was told them."* (Luke 2:8-20)

Angels told the shepherds about Jesus. Shepherds were at that time were considered lowly in society, yet the angels came and told the shepherds anyway. Angels are messengers. You are to be a messenger and tell everyone about Jesus, even those not considered highly esteemed by the world. This includes, the homeless, those in prison, those with disabilities.... When the shepherds learned about Jesus, they made haste to find Him. When you first learn about Jesus, don't waste time, make haste to seek him out. Once you have an encounter with Jesus, you must praise and glorify Him to others.

When my wife and I were doing ministry in Pine Hills, Florida, there was a homeless man that we encountered. He was always walking the streets intoxicated, sometimes with different shoes on or no shoes at all. We ministered to him, got him help, gave him food, invited him to church and we told him about Jesus. A few weeks later, some people came to church that we had never met. We asked them how they heard of our church, they said, "a man with two different shoes on had told them to come to our church." Amazing, more than two thousand years later, the Bible is proven true once again.

The Flight into Egypt

"The Bible says, *"Now when they had departed, behold, an angel of the Lord appeared to Joseph in a dream, saying, "Arise, take the young Child and His mother, flee to Egypt, and stay there until I bring you word; for Herod will seek the young Child to destroy Him."* (Matthew 2:13-18)

Once again, God spoke in a dream. Joseph was warned to protect Jesus. Joseph obeyed. He and Mary took Jesus and fled to Egypt where Jesus would be safe. You are to protect Jesus at all costs, even if it means it is an inconvenience. You may have to uproot your life for a time, but you must protect Jesus from a world that wants to destroy Him.

Simeon Sees Jesus

There is a part of the Christmas Story that gets left out and includes a man named Simeon. It had been revealed to Simeon that he would not see death before he had seen the Messiah.

The Bible says, *"A man named Simeon lived in Jerusalem. He was a good man who was devoted to God. He was waiting for the time when God would come to help Israel. The Holy Spirit was with him. The Holy Spirit told him that he would not die before he saw the Messiah from the Lord. The Spirit led Simeon to the Temple. So he was there when Mary and Joseph brought the baby Jesus to do what the Jewish law said they must do. Simeon took the baby in his arms and thanked God: "Now, Lord, you can let me, your servant, die in peace as you said. I have seen with my own eyes how you will save your people. Now all people can see your plan. He is a light to show your way to the other nations. And he will bring honor to your people Israel." Jesus' father and mother were amazed at what Simeon said about him. Then Simeon blessed them and said to Mary, "Many Jews will fall and many will rise because of this boy. He will be a sign from God that some will not accept. So the secret thoughts of many will be made known. And the things that happen will be painful for you—like a sword cutting through your heart."* (Luke 2:25-35)

Joseph and Mary brought Jesus to the temple. This is an example for us. When you go to church or wherever you go, bring Jesus with you. Do not leave Him behind or go halfhearted. Let His light shine and let others see Jesus in you. There are people you will encounter that need the Lord. You are to bring Jesus to others, so they can have an encounter with Him before they die.

Lastly, Simeon gives a prophecy of what is to come. Simeon said, *"So the secret thoughts of many will be made known."* This means that His treatment will bring to light the secret thoughts of people. Simeon also said, *"And the things that happen will be painful for you—like a sword cutting through your heart."* This is a prophecy of the pain Mary would endure witnessing the crucifixion of Jesus. We as believers, will also see things after we deliver Jesus to the world that will be painful. We will see Christ and His followers being persecuted and crucified even today by the world.

The Christmas Story: God's Instruction Manual for the Gift of Jesus

God wants you to receive Jesus within you and deliver Him to the world. You must be obedient even if you face ridicule, persecution or death and you must go anywhere God calls you. While you are delivering Jesus to the world, you cannot forsake your responsibilities to society. You must tell everyone about Jesus, including those not regarded highly in society and make haste to seek Him out for yourself. You must protect Jesus from the world that wishes to eliminate Him, even if it means inconvenience in your life You must listen and be obedient to God and ignore the instructions of the world. Lastly, you must bring Jesus to others, so they can have an encounter with Him before they die.

How the World Treats the Gift of Jesus

The Christmas Story is the instruction manual for how believers are to handle the gift of Jesus. Let me explain how the world handles the gift of Jesus. The scriptures regarding the arrest, trial, scourging and crucifixion of Jesus is what the world wants to do to Jesus, even still today. It is a direct contrast to the Christmas Story.

First, the world rejects Jesus. They do not accept this gift, because they do not believe He is the Messiah. They do not protect Him, they accuse Him and put Him on trial even though he is innocent. They scourge Him, (disfigure and alter his appearance) so he is not recognizable. Lastly, they try to put him to death, eliminate him from society. However, no matter how hard the world tries, they cannot kill Jesus. The good news is that Jesus rose from dead and He is alive today.

EPILOGUE
THE SINNER'S PRAYER

Accept Jesus as your Lord and Savior and it will break you free of the bondage of Satan and bring eternal life. All you must do is say the sinner's prayer. I will allow the words of Reverend Franklin Graham to lead you in this prayer. When his father, Reverend Billy Graham, went on to be with the Lord, my wife and I traveled from Florida to North Carolina to attend the wake to pay our respects. The following are the words spoken by Franklin Graham at the funeral service.

"Jesus tells us that no one comes to the Father except through Him. The world with all of its political correctness would want you to believe that there are many roads to God. It's just not true. How could Jesus make these claims? How could he say that He's the Way, the Truth, and the Life, and no man comes to the Father but by Him? You see, Jesus was God in the flesh, because He is the only one in history to take our sins and to pay the debt of sin, and my father would want me to share this with you today, that God sent His Son, His only Son, from Heaven to this Earth to take our sins, and he took our sins to the cross, and he died in our place. He shed His blood for each and every one of you, and when He hung on the cross God poured out the sins of mankind on His Son; the sins past, present, future. He shed His blood for our sins. He was buried for our sins, and on the third day God raised His Son to life. Jesus is not dead. He is alive, and He's here today. Are you trusting Him? He'll come into each and every heart that invites Him, and if we repent of our sins and by faith believe on the Name of the Lord Jesus Christ the Bible says we will be saved. Are you saved? Are you forgiven? Are you trusting Jesus as Your Savior? Are you following Him as your

Lord? If you're not sure there'd be no better time than right now at Billy Graham's funeral to settle this once and for eternity. It's simply by faith, simply by believing, and if you were just to pray a simple prayer like this, just say in your heart, just say this in your heart, "God, I'm a sinner. I'm sorry for my sins. Forgive me. I believe that Jesus Christ is Your Son, and I want to trust Him as my Savior, and I want to follow Him as my Lord." If you just pray a simple prayer like that God will forgive your sins, and you can have that hope of eternal life. It's simply by faith, simply by believing, and if you were just to pray a simple prayer like this, just say in your heart, just say this in your heart, "God, I'm a sinner. I'm sorry for my sins. Forgive me. I believe that Jesus Christ is Your Son, and I want to trust Him as my Savior, and I want to follow Him as my Lord." If you just pray a simple prayer like that God will forgive your sins, and you can have that hope of eternal life." Reverend Franklin Graham

ABOUT THE AUTHOR

I was blessed to be raised by loving parents that believed in God. When I was young, my parents would bring me to church. It was a Greek church and much of the service was not in English, so I did not understand a lot. After high school, I attended the University of Central Florida where I sought out the world as most young people do. I graduated with a degree in finance and began a career in financial services. I worked for companies like Morgan Stanley, JP Morgan Chase, The Bank of New York and E*TRADE. I was working very long hours, living for things to satisfy my flesh and to show others that I was successful. In order to improve myself and advance my career, I read self-help books on success. One day, I purchase a book called the Power of Positive Thinking by Norman Vincent Peale. I had no idea that he was a pastor. On one of the first few pages, he talked about writing down an affirmation for someone that he was counseling. It was the scripture, *"I can do all things through Christ who strengthens me."* It was like a shockwave went through my system. God ignited something in me that started when I was young when my parents brought me to church.

While I was working at E*TRADE and lived in Atlanta, I would drive to Florida to see my parents. During my drive, I searched the radio stations for something to listen to. One day, I heard this man speaking very eloquently. His voice was lovely, and the message was beautiful. I later learned it was Dr. David Jeremiah. When I moved back to Florida about a year later, I was working for a bank and a friend invited me to church. One Sunday morning, I got up, decided to keep my word to my friend and I went to church. My life changed forever… I loved it and I never looked back! I was baptized, and I joined the church. Over the next two years, I never missed a service.

I was never truly happy when I was in the world. I was single, never married and had no children. My life was being wasted on a selfish existence and keeping up appearances. My life had no meaning and was built on possessions. Everything the world was teaching me was wrong.

I eventually met my wife while serving in the church. She had a lady's ministry in one of the largest churches in Orlando. I helped her in ministry for many years and I grew in the things of God. I left the world of financial services and began working with individuals with developmental disabilities. In time, my wife and I planted our own church in Pine Hills, Florida. It was the greatest and most rewarding experience of my life. My message to you, life will present you with many twists and turns. Never lose heart! Where you are right now is not were you will end up... However, you must turn from the world and turn to the Lord. The Bible says, *"But seek first the kingdom of God and His righteousness, and all these things shall be added to you."* (Matthew 6:33)